Beside Still Waters

Beside Still Waters

David R. Veerman

with calligraphy by *Timothy R. Botts*

Tyndale House Publishers, Inc.
WHEATON, ILLINOIS

Library of Congress Cataloging-in-Publication Data

Veerman, David.
  Beside still waters / David R. Veerman.
    p.   cm.
   ISBN 0-8423-0119-4 (pbk. : alk. paper)
    1. Devotional calendars. 2. Bible—Meditations. 3. Meditations.
I. Title.
BV4811.V44 1996
242'.2—dc20   96-25642

Printed in the United States of America

02 01 00 99 98 97 96
9 8 7 6 5 4 3 2 1

So God created people

in his own image;

God patterned them

after himself;

male and female

he created them.

GENESIS 1:27

A

"You're nothing!" "You're useless!"

WHETHER shouted, spoken, or implied, those cutting statements wound deeply. And even if you've never heard those specific words, you can feel useless, unwanted, and worthless.

Left out. Ridiculed. Put down. Overlooked. Forgotten. Lost in the crowd.

But this verse, nestled in the first chapter of the first book of God's Word, shouts the opposite. You have value. You count! As a descendent of the first parents, you are God's special creation, made in his image. Thus, in some way, you are like God. And if you think this verse is too good to be true, read the rest of the Bible. You will discover covenant promises, redemption, grace, mercy, forgiveness, salvation, and guidance.

Regardless of painful circumstances and hateful words, know that you have worth. God created you, and he loves you. Let that truth sink into your soul, and then bask in his love and live as his special child.

B

Then the LORD said to Abraham,

"Why did Sarah laugh? Why did she say,

'Can an old woman like me have a baby?'

Is anything too hard for the LORD?

About a year from now, just as I told you,

I will return, and Sarah will have a son."

GENESIS 18:13-14

IS ANYTHING TOO

NEARLY one hundred years old, Abraham and Sarah were astounded at God's announcement that they would have a son. Decades beyond childbearing years, Sarah chuckled at the prospect, thinking the promise impossible to fulfill. So God had to remind them that *nothing* was too hard for him. And true to God's word, one year later Isaac ("laughter") was born.

Two great truths emerge from this incident: (1) God can do anything—nothing is "too hard for the Lord"—and (2) God keeps his promises.

What "too hard" task do you face? If God wants you to do it, you can, *with him*—nothing is "too hard for the Lord."

What impossible obstacle lies in your path? If God wants you to move it, you can, *with him*—"with God everything is possible" (Matthew 19:26).

What amazing promise has God given you? He will do it.

Stop wondering, worrying, and doubting—and start living.

With unfailing love

you will lead this people

whom you have ransomed.

You will guide them in your strength

to the place where

your holiness dwells.

EXODUS 15:13

FOLLOW

AFTER having endured decades of slavery and then having watched seven plagues devastate the country while Pharaoh's heart hardened before their eyes, the children of Israel had finally been allowed to leave Egypt, to travel to their Promised Land. Yet, looking back from the edge of the Red Sea, they saw the dust kicked up by the horses of the Egyptian army—Pharaoh had again changed his mind and was pursuing with deadly intent.

But God parted the waters, and they walked to freedom on dry ground. Soon thereafter, God released the waters and drowned the pursuing army.

What a relief! What joy! What gratitude! Moses and Miriam led the people in praise to God who had delivered them. This verse is a small portion of their song.

Who stands as your Pharaoh, enslaving you while defying God? Where lies your Egypt from which you dream of escape? Remember that your Lord fights your battles and will lead you through the deep waters to your promised land. Praise him for his strength and guidance, and step into the sea.

YOUR LEADER

Then I will remember my covenant

with Jacob, with Isaac, and with Abraham,

and I will remember the land. . . .

I will remember my ancient covenant

with their ancestors,

whom I brought out of Egypt

while all the nations watched.

I, the LORD, am their God.

LEVITICUS 26:42, 45

GOD

TWICE in these two verses, God refers to his covenant, and three times he says that he will remember.

People forget. We forget names, places, and even promises. We even use forgetting as an excuse, as in "Sorry, I forgot."

But God remembers. He remembers people (Isaac, Abraham, the people's ancestors), places ("the land"), and especially his covenant promises. And he remembers *you*.

Do you ever feel forgotten—lost in the crowd, in the increasing pace of life, or even in the culture of the corporation? Feeling lonely and anonymous, you may wonder whether anybody knows or cares.

God does. He remembers your name and his promise to be with you, to guide you, and to bring you home.

Now it's up to you to remember . . .
your Lord and his love for you . . .
and then to find hope in him.

REMEMBERS

Instruct Aaron and his sons to bless

the people of Israel with this special blessing:

"May the LORD bless you and protect you.

May the LORD smile on you and be gracious to you.

May the LORD show you his favor

and give you his peace."

This is how Aaron and his sons

will designate the Israelites as my people,

and I myself will bless them.

NUMBERS 6:23-27

GO IN

*T*HIS familiar benediction often graces church services. Whether sung by the choir or pronounced by the pastor, it gives the congregation a comfortable, warm feeling as they exit. Unfortunately, much like the expression "God bless you" after a sneeze, this benediction has become trivialized by familiarity. We really don't think much about how we are being "blessed."

But consider these statements:

- *protect you*—requesting God's protection and guidance
- *smile on you*—requesting a close, loving relationship with God
- *be gracious*—requesting that God would shower his forgiveness and kindness upon you, though unearned and undeserved
- *give you his peace*—requesting inner strength, resolve, and confidence for living in tumultuous times

Certainly this blessing of the Israelites through Moses, Aaron, and Aaron's sons contains much of what we really want God to do in our lives. But the key statement lies in the last line: This "will designate the Israelites as my people."

Do you belong to God? Do you bear his name? This passage is for you. Know that you are *blessed.*

PEACE

Listen to me, all you men of Israel!

Do not be afraid as you go out to fight today!

Do not lose heart or panic.

For the LORD your God is going with you!

He will fight for you against your enemies,

and he will give you victory!

DEUTERONOMY 20:3-4

CLAIM THE

GOD told the priest to explain to the people that the one who had brought them out of Egypt was always with them. Regardless of the enemy, they need not fear because God would fight with them and for them, assuring them of victory.

Enemies continue to threaten God's people: financial struggles, failing health, job stress, family conflict, persecution. Normal reactions to such daunting battles include frustration, fear, and, often, outright terror. Instead, God tells us to recall his previous work—past assurances of his presence and demonstrations of his power—and to know that this same powerful and loving God is with us *today,* in *this* battle.

What enemy do you face? Don't panic. God is still all-powerful, and he loves you. God brought you through before, and he will do it again. He stands on *your* side, fighting for you and with you.

Know who marches with you, and move forward in faith.

The eternal God is your refuge,

and his everlasting arms are under you.

He thrusts out the enemy before you;

it is he who cries,

"Destroy them!"

DEUTERONOMY 33:27

7

*J*UST before Israel moved into the Promised Land and just before Moses' death, Moses blessed the nation of Israel (see Deuteronomy 33:1). This blessing for the tribe of Asher promises that God will keep them safe, held securely in his "everlasting arms."

Picture a muscular young shepherd carrying a frightened lamb through a storm, above swirling river waters, to the safety of the fold. The shepherd's steps are sure, and his hold on the lamb is strong.

Or picture a father lifting his child and pulling her close in a loving embrace, wiping her tears and assuring her that all is well.

That's God—loving, strong, and always there. His "arms" hold us securely and eternally. They never let go.

What enemies threaten you today? What dangers surround you? Live by faith, confidently resting in your Father's "everlasting arms."

No one will be able

to stand their ground against you

as long as you live.

For I will be with you as I was with Moses.

I will not fail you or abandon you.

JOSHUA 1:5

GOD IS WITH YOU

8

POISED to assume the leadership of God's people, Joshua must have nervously wondered if he was up to such an awesome task. Besides the great responsibility of being the political and military leader, like a president or other head of state today, Joshua also served as spiritual leader. His job was to lead God's people into the Promised Land, to keep them focused on the Lord as they settled the land and organized as a nation.

Joshua would also know the great price of leadership—loneliness. He alone would stand as the leader; he alone would bear the responsibility. No one else would be able to take credit for success or blame for failure.

At this critical time of transition, God spoke to Joshua, assuring him of his presence and power.

And God's word to his man has echoed through time as a word of assurance to all of his people: *I will not fail you or abandon you.* (See also Deuteronomy 31:6; 31:8; Hebrews 13:5.)

God has called you to leadership—in your home, on the job, in the community, or at church. As you plan, organize, and motivate, know that you don't lead alone—God stands with you. And when those lonely times come, know that you are not alone—God will never abandon you.

No one is holy like the LORD!

There is no one besides you;

there is no Rock like our God.

1 SAMUEL 2:2

ANNAH needed a miracle. Desperately wanting a child, she prayed and asked God to give her a son. And she vowed to dedicate this child to the Lord and to his service. God answered Hannah's request, and Hannah kept her promise. These words are from her dedication prayer.

Filled with joy and gratitude, Hannah prayed. She was thrilled with her new situation—the mother of a miracle child—yet she rejoiced not in what had happened to her but in who God was. Notice that Hannah's prayer highlights God's holiness, proclaiming that no one like God exists; in fact, no one is even close. God's perfection, presence, and power place him far beyond others.

Next, she exclaimed that God stood as the greatest "Rock." This pictures God as solid and secure, but it also implies safety. People would run to the rocks for cover and protection. Hannah knew God to be rock solid and a secure haven for her soul.

When you feel desperate and hope for a miracle, to whom do you turn? Only God can meet your deepest needs.

But the LORD said to Samuel,

"Don't judge by his appearance or height,

for I have rejected him.

The LORD doesn't make decisions the way you do!

People judge by outward appearance,

but the LORD looks at a person's

thoughts and intentions."

1 SAMUEL 16:7

YOU ARE

GOD sent Samuel to Bethlehem, to the house of Jesse, to anoint one of Jesse's sons as the next king of Israel. It would have been quite understandable for Samuel to assume that the next king would be tall, handsome, and strong like Israel's first king, Saul. Isn't that how kings are supposed to be?

"But the Lord looks at a person's thoughts and intentions."

The next king would not be Eliab, Abinadab, Shammah, or any of the seven older boys. Instead, God chose the youngest son—David the shepherd boy.

Over the centuries, society has continued to value superficial appearances. Plaudits and power still come to the beautiful people—sports stars and media celebrities with exceptional physical characteristics. With such men and women presented as ideals and models, it's easy for the rest of us to feel ugly, unwanted, insignificant, and worthless in comparison.

But God's standards have not changed. Rather than outward appearance, he looks at the inside of a person, examining thoughts and intentions—desires, motives, character, attitudes, and faith.

Expend your energy on developing inner beauty. That's what matters to God. And his opinion is all that really counts.

BEAUTIFUL

People
outward

*judge by
appearance*

BUT
THE LORD
LOOKS AT a Person's thoughts
and intentions

from 1 SAMUEL 16:7

The LORD is my rock,

my fortress, and my savior;

my God is my rock, in whom I find protection.

He is my shield, the strength of my salvation,

and my stronghold, my high tower, my savior,

the one who saves me from violence.

I will call on the LORD,

who is worthy of praise,

for he saves me from my enemies.

2 SAMUEL 22:2-4

ROCK

TODDLERS clutch blankets, cloth diapers, stuffed toys, and other security symbols, dragging them wherever they go. They're cute, but that's because they're babies. Older children, teenagers, and adults with similar actions would be seen as mentally slow or emotionally weak. Yet today, many adults tightly clutch other, socially acceptable, "security blankets": a special relationship, fame, good health, a prestigious career, talent, prized possessions, money. Some security! Each one of these "blankets" can be lost, stolen, or swept away, and each will fail when needed most.

In contrast, listen to these words of David as he describes his source of security: "rock," "fortress," "savior," "shield," "stronghold," "high tower." David knew from personal experience that *God alone* could secure his present and his future.

What are you holding? On what are you depending? Build your life on the *rock*—God almighty. He's the only secure foundation.

"Don't be afraid!"

Elisha told him.

"For there are more on our side

than on theirs!"

2 KINGS 6:16

CLAIM THE

THE ARAMEANS had surrounded Dothan in an attempt to capture Elisha. When Elisha's servant discovered the enemy encamped around them, he exclaimed with fear, "Ah, my lord, what will we do now?" (2 Kings 6:15). That's when Elisha told him, "There are more on our side than on theirs!"

Then, with his eyes opened by God, the servant looked again and saw the hills full of horses and chariots of fire—God's angelic army—encircling the enemy (6:17). Victory was assured!

Often enemies surround us. At times the opposing forces have faces and names—coworkers, neighbors, unbelievers who would deny faith. Often, however, the enemy is unseen but just as real—satanic forces seeking to defeat the spirit, steal hope and joy, and ruin lives. That's when believers need eyes of faith to see God's infinite power and his mighty hosts encircling the enemy and guaranteeing victory.

Look at your enemies. Now look again. See God at work on your behalf. See the hosts of heaven on your side. Then, with victory assured, live with confidence and serve your commander in chief.

Give thanks to the LORD

and proclaim his greatness.

Let the whole world know

what he has done.

1 CHRONICLES 16:8

REJOICE IN

EMORIES are selective. People often long for "the good old days" when, in reality, those days were not very good at all. Others carry a grudge for years, recalling bitterly a past insult or wrong. Some conveniently forget a promise or commitment as they seek personal gratification. And most people tend to forget God—who he is and what he has done.

In this stirring psalm, David urges the people to remember the Lord, his wonders, miracles, and judgments. David's point seems to be that if we focus on the person, commandments, and works of God, we will praise him, seek him, live for him, and tell others about him. And we certainly won't despair when life gets rough.

How's your memory? Make a habit of thanking and praising God each day for who he is, what he has done, and what he has promised. Then tell others of his faithfulness.

Stand up and praise the LORD your God,

for he lives from everlasting to everlasting! . . .

Praise his glorious name!

It is far greater than we can think or say.

You alone are the LORD.

You made the skies and the heavens

and all the stars.

You made the earth and the seas

and everything in them.

You preserve and give life to everything,

and all the angels of heaven worship you.

NEHEMIAH 9:5-6

WORSHIP

NEHEMIAH had returned to Jerusalem. With courage, tenacity, and strong leadership, he organized the people to rebuild the city walls. Afterward, they worshiped God together.

It was a remarkable scene, actually. As Ezra read from the Book of the Law, many wept, realizing that they had been living far below God's standards. (For some, it was the *first* time they had ever understood God's Word.) Then, after confessing their sins, they praised their eternal and glorious Lord for his love, forgiveness, and work in their lives.

Genuine worship and praise overflow from a grateful heart. When people truly understand the gravity of their sin and the depth of God's love, they cannot help but stand and shout praises to the Lord. And they make the changes in their lives that God requires.

If your fervor has cooled or you feel far from God, reread passages in his Word to remind you of his nature and his work. Then join the "angels of heaven"— *Stand up and praise the Lord your God, for he lives from everlasting to everlasting!*

I know that my Redeemer lives,

and that he will stand upon the earth at last.

And after my body has decayed,

yet in my body I will see God!

I will see him for myself.

Yes, I will see him with my own eyes.

I am overwhelmed at the thought!

JOB 19:25-27

SEE WITH EYES

Look to the Lord

CONSIDER Job's condition. He had lost all of his children, livestock, and possessions. Everything had been taken except his wife, who had reacted by telling him to "curse God and die" (Job 2:9). Next, he became afflicted with boils. Then his friends showed up and, after a time of silence, began spewing mindless counsel and accusations of unnamed sins. What devastating pain and loneliness! The natural reaction would have been to become embittered and take his wife's advice.

But Job's faith was rooted in God—not in his situation or surroundings. He knew that his Redeemer was alive and in control. Despite Job's terrible physical and emotional pain, he could look beyond his circumstances to the Lord and beyond his present condition to the future.

Few, if any, have suffered as much as Job did. Few, if any, have expressed such deep faith.

What pain do you endure? Learn with Job that God can meet you in your need. As Corrie ten Boom stated, "No matter how deep the pit, God is deeper still."

O LORD, I have so many enemies;

so many are against me.

So many are saying,

"God will never rescue him!"

But you, O LORD, are a shield around me,

my glory,

and the one who lifts my head high.

PSALM 3:1-3

GOD WILL

DAVID wrote this psalm while fleeing from Absalom. With his own son turning against him, David seemed to be surrounded by enemies. Even those who stood on his side expressed pessimism concerning the eventual outcome, doubting that even God could save him. Certainly David could have become utterly discouraged and without hope.

Yet he confidently wrote that God would protect him, destroy his enemies, and restore him to his rightful place on the throne. David had no idea *how* this would happen—he was devastated politically, physically, and emotionally. But he knew *who* was in charge of his life and destiny. David's confidence rested not on his abilities or the strength of his armies but on his sovereign God.

Many seem to spend their lives running and hiding, upset about the past, anxious about the present, and worried about the future. Seeing enemies everywhere, even in themselves, they hang their heads in shame and despair. David could have given up; instead, he found courage and hope in God.

God is your shield, too. Trust him. He will bestow glory upon you and lift your head high.

DELIVER YOU

I will lie down

in peace and sleep,

for you alone, O LORD,

will keep me safe.

PSALM 4:8

FOR MONTHS, David was harassed in the palace and then chased through the desert by King Saul. Later, during his own reign as king, David faced a host of enemies, both from outside Israel's borders and from within. Eventually, even his own sons Absalom and Adonijah tried to overthrow him. David must have often feared for his safety as he encountered enemies at every turn.

Instead of being paralyzed by fear, David ruled confidently, secure in his relationship with his loving heavenly Father. In this song David writes that he could "lie down in peace and sleep" because God would protect him.

You, like David, may be surrounded by enemies who are intent on causing you great harm. Perhaps even loved ones have turned against you. And, if you're honest, you might have to admit that sleep has not come easily at night, with anxieties and fears filling your dreams. You may even fear for your life.

If so, check out David's cure for insomnia—his secret for sleeping "in peace." The secret? David focused his attention on his Lord instead of on his situation, remembering God's power and love. And he prayed about his situation and his worries (Psalm 4:1).

Only God can keep you safe.

SECURITY

Listen to my voice

in the morning, LORD.

Each morning

I bring my requests to you

and wait expectantly.

PSALM 5:3

GOD HEARS

ACH MORNING, David would spend time with the Lord, worshiping him and presenting needs. Then David would "wait," fully expecting God to fulfill his requests. David wasn't simply moving through a daily religious ritual. Confident that God was listening, he had very personal discussions with his loving Father. David's relationship with God was close and personal, so he could "wait expectantly."

Although God wants his people to talk with him continually through the day (see 1 Thessalonians 5:16-18), we need special times of deep conversation with him, confessing our sins, sharing our feelings, and presenting our requests. Spending time with God in the morning gives us the whole day to think about the conversation and to watch him answer our prayers.

Whenever you talk with God, know that he is listening—he hears your voice. Share your thoughts, feelings, and needs with him, and expect him to answer.

When I look at the night sky

and see the work of your fingers—

the moon and the stars

you have set in place—

what are mortals that you should think of us,

mere humans that you should care for us?

For you made us only a little lower than God,

and you crowned us with glory and honor.

PSALM 8:3-5

19

DO YOU FEEL small and insignificant when you look up at the night sky and the expanse of stars? When you look down at the countless lights of an urban sprawl? When you look around at an assembled throng?

David had that feeling; yet he understood that in God's eyes he was important, created just a little lower than God himself.

Truthfully, every person, including you, has significance as God's special creation, "crowned with glory and honor."

Take another look, a closer look, at the moon and stars, and see the truth—the Creator of all that exists cares about you and is thinking about you. You are significant; you are not lost in the cosmos or crowd.

Then, look at yourself as God does.

For the needy

will not be forgotten forever;

the hopes of the poor

will not always be crushed.

PSALM 9:18

REMEMBERED

20

REMEMBER when you were a child and became separated from your mother in the department store? All you saw were tall strangers and merchandise stacked to the ceiling as you panicked and rushed from aisle to aisle. Nothing is as frightening as the feeling of being lost or abandoned.

Although you are now a grown-up, still you can feel forgotten and lost, especially when most people seem to be obsessed with themselves, their personal comfort, and pleasure. They rush by, ignoring you and *your* needs.

That feeling of abandonment intensifies when the needs for food, shelter, and companionship scream out to be met or when a person is afflicted by illness, persecution, or natural catastrophe. Weak and nearly helpless, that person feels vulnerable and afraid.

But listen to this psalm, which underscores a great promise from our loving Lord. Although you may be virtually invisible in this world, God sees you—he has not forgotten. Although the future looks dismal today, God continues to give you his promise of bright tomorrows.

You are not lost—look up and find God. And look ahead, to eternity, and find hope.

THE

LORD

REACHED

DOWN

He led me e

FROM

He rescued me

HEAVEN

AND

to a place of safety.

because he delights in me

RESCUED
ME

HE DREW ME
OUT OF
DEEP
WATERS

from PSALM 18:16,19

He reached down from heaven and rescued me;

he drew me out of deep waters.

He delivered me from my powerful enemies,

from those who hated me and

were too strong for me.

They attacked me at a moment

when I was weakest,

but the LORD upheld me.

He led me to a place of safety;

he rescued me because he delights in me.

PSALM 18:16-19

HE DELIGHTS

21

DAVID sang this psalm after God had rescued him from vindictive King Saul. Although David had few resources and allies, he knew that God would protect and defend him. Certainly David's enemies were "powerful" and "too strong" for him. Trying to defeat them on his own surely would have led to disaster. So David found his strength in almighty God.

Then, having been delivered from Saul, David expressed his deep gratitude to the Lord for his love and care. In this poetic song, David pictures God as reaching down from heaven, plucking him from a raging sea, and setting him on solid and dry ground. Why would God do such a thing? "Because," David answers, "he delights in me."

Few today are pursued by embittered kings and their armies. At times, however, you may feel like David, surrounded by powerful enemies. With victory impossible on your own and with no way out, your only hope is in the Lord. Ask for his help; look for his guidance and direction; depend on his strength. And, after the rescue, praise his name!

The law of the LORD is perfect, reviving the soul.

The decrees of the LORD are trustworthy,

making wise the simple.

The commandments of the LORD are right,

bringing joy to the heart.

The commands of the LORD are clear,

giving insight to life.

Reverence for the LORD is pure, lasting forever.

The laws of the LORD are true; each one is fair.

PSALM 19:7-9

22

- Do you want to know what God wants? Read his book.
- Do you want to know how to please God? Read the Scriptures.
- Do you want to know how to live? Read God's Word.

CHECK OUT God's law, statutes, precepts, commands, and ordinances. They are "perfect," "trustworthy," "right," "clear," and "pure." And following them will bring revival, wisdom, joy, and insight!

Don't lose your way in the fog of worldly values and human understanding. Study God's message, learn his truths, and follow his instruction; then you will stay on the right road and move in the right direction.

The LORD is my shepherd;

I have everything I need.

He lets me rest in green meadows;

he leads me beside peaceful streams.

He renews my strength.

PSALM 23:1-3

STILL WATERS,

23

THE TRADITIONAL READING of this last sentence is "He restoreth my soul."

Restoring an antique requires paint remover, hard work, and patience. Restoring an old house requires masonry, carpentry, plumbing, electrical skills, and a considerable investment of time, money, and energy. But what does it take to restore a soul?

When trials and time join forces to ravage us, tearing at body and mind and crushing the spirit, we desperately need restoration—to be refreshed and renewed and brought back to mint condition. But only the Lord can do that work. As our original designer and creator, only he knows us and has the tools. Only he can restore our souls.

God begins his miracle of restoration by leading us, like a caring shepherd, away from the bustle and traffic, stress and storms, to the green meadows where we can rest and eat. And he leads us to the peaceful streams, the still waters—calm, quiet, deep, inviting—where we can quench our thirst and receive his loving care.

Renewal begins when we, like frightened sheep, stop running and struggling and submit to our Shepherd. God wants to restore our souls, and he has everything we need.

Surely your goodness

and unfailing love

will pursue me all the days of my life,

and I will live in the house

of the LORD forever.

PSALM 23:6

NO TRIVIAL

24

*M*ANY of us learned the Twenty-third Psalm in the King James Version, which says that "goodness and mercy shall follow me. . . ." But the Hebrew word actually means "pursue," as in this translation. In other words, David is saying that God's goodness and love will chase after him, *aggressively* following him "all the days" of his life.

What a beautiful picture and encouraging promise for those who belong to the Lord—we can never outrun his love, and he runs right behind us every step of the way. This means that . . .

- If everyone deserts, leaving us virtually alone, God will be with us.
- Wherever we are and whatever we are going through, God's love will be there.
- Regardless of the evil in the world, God's goodness will come through.

And the ultimate result of God's pursuing us with his goodness and love is life with our Lord, *forever!*

If, in running through a hectic and pressure-packed life, you lose sight of God, turn around—he is there.

Wait patiently for the LORD.

Be brave and courageous.

Yes, wait patiently

for the LORD.

PSALM 27:14

25

*W*AITING is difficult in a hurried, fast-paced world. Waiting is frustrating for impatient people. We want answers and service and money and success and healing . . . NOW!

But God says to have patience, to wait for him and *his* timing.

That makes sense, of course. God knows us, he knows the future, and his timing is perfect. Of course we should wait. Of course we should endure. Of course we should listen for his voice and follow his guidance.

Instead, we rush headlong into life. Then we wonder why we struggle and fear.

Waiting for the Lord means recognizing his wisdom, admitting his sovereignty, and submitting to his control. Waiting involves prayer, talking to God about our dilemmas and decisions, and pouring out our feelings. But as we wait, God gives us strength and courage to meet the challenges before us.

Looking for a quick fix? immediate gratification? easy answers? Instead, wait for the Lord.

The LORD says,

"I will guide you along the best pathway

for your life.

I will advise you and

watch over you."

PSALM 32:8

MAKE THE

26

CHILDREN think they know just about everything. One junior high student recently remarked that he didn't need to go to church because he knew "all the stories." Adolescents are known for their cocky self-assuredness.

The older we get, however, the more we realize how little knowledge we actually possess. We find that we have more and more questions and fewer and fewer answers. Instead of being black and white, life seems filled with gray areas. We struggle with complex issues and problems that have no obvious solutions. We wonder what to do, which way to turn, how to live, and where to go. And we doubt.

Thus, God's promise in this psalm gives us hope. Note that he doesn't offer simple solutions and easy answers; he offers himself. God says he will *guide, advise,* and *watch.* In other words, God will help us go in the right direction and then protect us on the road.

That's great news to finite, confused, and doubting human beings because it comes from the infinite, all-knowing, and all-powerful creator and ruler of the universe.

What life issues boggle your mind? What decisions slow you down? What problems harass your steps? Look to the Lord for guidance. He won't zap you to your destination, but he will guide you along the way.

How precious is

your unfailing love, O God!

All humanity finds shelter in the shadow

of your wings.

You feed them from the abundance

of your own house,

letting them drink from your rivers of delight.

For you are the fountain of life,

the light by which we see.

PSALM 36:7-9

GOD LOVES

27

GOD'S priceless love cannot be bought, not with money, good works, or any other commodity. It is free and available to all who trust in him: men, women, rich, poor, powerful, and powerless—"all humanity." In this psalm, David uses a variety of images to describe the meaning of this profound truth:

- *shelter in the shadow of your wings*—like a baby bird who finds safety in the nest, we are protected by God.
- *feed them from the abundance of your own house*—God invites us as welcomed guests to his lavish banquet table overflowing with blessings.
- *drink from your rivers of delight*—God's endless river brings refreshing, thirst-quenching joy.
- *you are the fountain of life*—God is the only source of eternal life, and we can know him!
- *the light by which we see*—God brings us out of darkness and reveals truth.

The picture is clear—God's love never fails, and you can know it . . . now.

I waited patiently for the LORD to help me,

and he turned to me and heard my cry.

He lifted me out of the pit of despair,

out of the mud and the mire.

He set my feet on solid ground and

steadied me as I walked along.

PSALM 40:1-2

GOD HEARS

28

WAITING takes patience, especially when we want answers and help immediately. And pain, problems, and pressures increase the difficulty—minutes can seem like days and hours like weeks.

We don't know the nature of the struggle that David faced before he finally heard from God. "Pit of despair," "mud," and "mire," seem to indicate, however, that it was extremely unpleasant. Yet David *waited patiently for the Lord.*

And David's patient reliance on God was rewarded.

Often God wants to teach us during those difficult times of waiting for answers, solutions, and resolutions. He wants us to learn that *he* is in control and that *he* alone is our sure foundation and ally.

Are you waiting for God's touch? for his answers? for his rescue? Keep crying for help, but in your cries, be patient. He will lift you up, set your feet on solid ground, and steady you as you walk.

Through each day

the LORD pours his unfailing love upon me,

and through each night I sing his songs,

praying to God who gives me life. . . .

Why am I discouraged? Why so sad?

I will put my hope in God!

I will praise him again—

my Savior and my God!

PSALM 42:8, 11

LOOK UP AND

29

AN UNSETTLING REPORT from the doctor, a lingering illness, a financial reversal, or a broken relationship—numerous setbacks and troubles can undermine our comfortable security and steal our dreams, causing us to be discouraged and sad and even to despair. Evidently something similar caused the writer of this psalm to lose heart.

But focusing on our great God can renew our strength and courage. The wonderful truth is that the loving Father directs our ways and guides each of our steps during the day. And at night, when we sleep, he still stands with us, watching and protecting. Thus, we see in this psalm that as the attention of the writer turns to God, discouragement transforms into hope and sorrow into praise.

What troubling questions, doubts, and struggles threaten and pester you? Take your eyes off your circumstances and turn to your Lord—look up instead of down. Then you will gain new hope, knowing that you are secure in God's loving arms.

Be silent,

and know that I am God!

I will be honored by every nation.

I will be honored throughout the world.

PSALM 46:10

BE SILENT

30

- "Stop!"
- "Be quiet!"
- "Let go of your concerns!"

THESE alternate translations for "be silent" fill in the picture. Through this psalm writer, God is telling us to take a significant break from the frantic pace and hectic schedule, to move away from society's deafening cacophony, to stop talking and start listening to him. Then, and only then, will we be positioned to get to know him, our eternal, all-powerful, all-knowing, ever present God.

It's not easy to disengage, to slow down, and to "be silent." Thirsting for success and hungering for meaning, we push and strain and fill every waking moment with noisy activity. And we work hard to succeed in our own strength, in our own power, under our own control.

But God will be "honored by every nation," and he will be "honored throughout the world." Right now, he wants to "be honored" in our lives.

Be silent—listen to God's gentle whisper.
Be silent—know that he alone is God.
Be silent—submit your way to him.

You are the fountain of life

THE LIGHT BY WHICH WE SEE

from PSALM 36:9

Give your burdens to the LORD,

and he will take care of you.

He will not permit the godly

to slip and fall.

PSALM 55:22

RELEASE

31

REMEMBER carrying a heavy bag on your shoulder? With every labored step, you seemed to bend a bit lower. Finally, upon reaching your destination, you summoned the strength, and with a push and a grunt you dropped the load where it belonged. What a relief! What a feeling of freedom!

Much like that great load, cares and anxieties often weigh us down, slowing our pace and stooping our shoulders. We worry about the future, finances, family, and friendships. We question past actions and fear coming events. No wonder ulcers, migraines, and insomnia are epidemic.

Instead of struggling under that overwhelming weight, however, God urges us to give our burdens to him. This pictures that last push where the bag is hoisted up and off the shoulder—"give your burdens to the Lord." God wants to free us to walk fearlessly and confidently, upright and strong, while *he* bears the load. He's strong enough to lift and carry anything we give him.

What heavy weight do you carry? What causes your sleepless nights and restless days? What pushes you to the brink? Let God carry your burdens—he will take care of you and keep you standing tall.

But when I am afraid,

I put my trust in you.

O God, I praise your word.

I trust in God, so why should I be afraid?

What can mere mortals do to me?

PSALM 56:3-4

32

THE FAMILIAR PHRASE stamped on all U.S. coins reads, "In God we trust." For most, that's merely a motto, a nice sentiment with very little basis in reality. But David had to put this into practice. Fleeing from Saul, he had taken refuge in Philistine territory. Thus, he had escaped from one enemy only to fall into the hands of another. From a purely human perspective, he was doomed—there was no way out.

Certainly David must have been afraid. Yet even in his fear he could affirm his strong trust in God. David knew God, and he knew that he could trust God's word. So the more David thought about his loving heavenly Father, the less he worried about his circumstances and his enemies. After all, what could "mere mortals" do to him?

How are you trusting these days? Are you nervous, anxious, concerned, fearful? Take a realistic look at your situation, but then look to God.

- He has the power.
- He has the will.
- He has your best interests at heart.
- He has strengthened you in the past.

Don't be afraid.

You are my strength;

I wait for you to rescue me,

for you, O God,

are my place of safety.

PSALM 59:9

GOD IS YOUR

33

KING SAUL had sent his men to capture and kill David. In the face of such deadly opposition and overwhelming odds, David could claim God as his place of safety and sing his praises.

Note that David wrote this psalm *before* being rescued. David's faith was unshakable. He trusted God to help him, but he knew that whatever happened, God, his "strength," controlled his fate. That was a truth he could live with.

God doesn't promise to deliver us from every threat, but he does promise his love and presence.

God doesn't promise us victory in every battle, but he does promise to work everything for our good.

God doesn't promise prosperity, but he does promise life eternal.

Regardless of the enemies that surround you, make God your strength and give him praise.

O God, listen to my cry! Hear my prayer!

From the ends of the earth,

I will cry to you for help,

for my heart is overwhelmed.

Lead me to the towering rock of safety.

PSALM 61:1-2

HE IS

34

REMEMBER when you drove away from home to go to college or to make your own way in the world? You watched your mother and father stand at the window and wave good-bye. They quickly became smaller and smaller until they disappeared from view.

At times that's how God seems—fading into the background, distant, beyond our understanding and experience.

Burdened by worries, overwhelmed by circumstances, besieged by temptation, or torn by guilt, we may forget his love and care as we speed on our way and put distance in the relationship.

Regardless of your location and situation, however, know that God is near. David called "from the ends of the earth" emotionally. No matter where you are—physically, emotionally, or morally—you can never be lost to God's love. You can call on him. He will listen to your prayer.

Praise the LORD;

praise God our savior!

For each day

he carries us in his arms.

PSALM 68:19

35

THE PSALMS of David overflow with praise. Having seen God work in his life—rescuing, protecting, guiding, strengthening, and forgiving—the musician-king David often wrote and sang of his deep gratitude to his loving Lord.

This song of David praises God as the one who daily carries us in his arms. The last part of this verse can also be translated "who daily bears our burdens"—a picture of God as our burden bearer, who carries the weight of sin, anxiety, and fear. What a relief to have those burdens lifted, to be set free from the heavy load that pushes us down.

Note also that David emphasizes that God bears these burdens and carries us *daily*. In other words, God doesn't take one load and then move on to something else. Each day, he carries the burdens of that day: Monday's important meeting at the office, Tuesday's assignment, Wednesday's relationship crisis, Thursday's health concern, Friday's decision, and so forth. Whatever we face, every day, we can turn it over to him—he will lift it onto his strong shoulders, giving us the freedom and strength to live for him.

What weighs you down? Thank God you have a burden bearer, and let him carry your load; let him carry you.

He will shield you with his wings.

He will shelter you with his feathers.

His faithful promises are

your armor and protection.

PSALM 91:4

THE LORD

36

THIS PSALM gives two pictures. The first is a powerful bird, sheltering her young with strong wings, holding the chicks close and standing between them and all threats to their safety.

The second is strong and sturdy armor, protecting a soldier in battle.

At times, we need shelter: refuge from winds, rain, floods, and other assaults. In the shelter we live in safety—warm, dry, and secure.

At times, we need armor to protect us from the attacks of those who would harm us: human enemies and spiritual forces, hateful and evil.

God provides our refuge, holding us close. And he provides the armor—his faithful promises.

When threats arise, seek shelter. In your battles, use your armor.

Praise the LORD, I tell myself;

with my whole heart, I will praise his holy name.

Praise the LORD, I tell myself,

and never forget the good things he does for me.

He forgives all my sins and heals all my diseases.

He ransoms me from death and surrounds me

with love and tender mercies.

He fills my life with good things.

My youth is renewed like the eagle's!

PSALM 103:1-5

PRAISE

37

*E*ACH YEAR we have a national day of "thanksgiving," a holiday set aside for remembering and counting all our blessings.

In this psalm, David, inspired by God's Spirit, proclaims his gratitude to God for all his "good things." Clearly this is a song of thanksgiving—David praising his wonderful Lord for who he is and for all his mighty works.

Consider each of the good things listed in light of what you are experiencing:

- *forgives all your sins*—Regardless of what you have done, God forgives through Christ Jesus your Lord.
- *heals all your diseases*—God brings you through the tough times and the pain.
- *ransoms you from death*—When you were sinking in sin, utterly without hope, God pulled you up and set your feet on solid ground. You have been rescued, redeemed, saved!
- *surrounds you with love and tender mercies*—God enfolds you with his love and compassion.
- *fills your life*—Whatever your struggle, God meets your need.
- *renews your youth*—When you feel weak and old, God gives you strength to continue living for him.

The LORD is like

a father to his children,

tender and compassionate

to those who fear him.

PSALM 103:13

YOUR LOVING

38

THROUGHOUT Scripture, God uses the word *father* to describe how he relates to his people. In this close and primary relationship, we learn about God and about fathering. Thus, we can know how a good father should act by looking at how God relates to his "children." Conversely, good human fathers provide a glimpse of God as they reflect his nature in their actions, as this psalm attests.

Good fathers have compassion on their children. They don't overpower with authority, lead by intimidation, respond with bitterness and spite, or enjoy meting out punishment. Instead, they empathize with their children, hurting when they hurt; they lead tenderly and firmly, with love and by example; they temper judgment with mercy, always being ready to forgive and start afresh.

God is the perfect example.

Have you trusted Christ as Savior? Do you call God "Father"? Do you "fear" (honor, respect, and obey) him? Then know that he deals with you with compassion. Admit your mistakes and frailties, and confess your sins. Run to his embrace; give him your hand; let him teach you his ways and lead you on the path of righteousness.

FATHER

I love the LORD

because he hears and answers my prayers.

Because he bends down and listens,

I will pray as long as I have breath!

PSALM 116:1-2

CALL ON

39

NEW MOTHERS seem to gain heightened hearing ability when their children are born. From three rooms away and through closed doors a mother can hear her baby's whimper. Everyone else is oblivious to the cry, so conversation continues. But the mother hears—her ears are tuned; her hearing is sensitive.

That's how the writer of this psalm pictures God. Bending down to listen to his people, God hears their cries, and he responds with mercy and grace.

It's easy to feel lost, alone, and anonymous in this noisy world where millions scream for attention. And when the pain strikes and tough times come, the lonely feelings grow . . . and we voice our silent pleas for help. Does anyone hear? Does anyone care?

God does. In fact, he "bends down and listens" to us. He hears the cry; he feels the pain; he sends his love.

In response to this great truth, the psalm writer professed his "love [for] the Lord" and promised to "pray as long as I have breath!"

What do you say? How will you respond?

The LORD protects those of childlike faith;

I was facing death, and then he saved me.

Now I can rest again,

for the LORD has been so good to me.

He has saved me from death,

my eyes from tears, my feet from stumbling.

And so I walk in the LORD's presence

as I live here on earth!

PSALM 116:6-9

IN HIS

40

*O*NE of the recurring themes of Psalms is God's loving protection. David and the other psalmists continually praised the Lord for his goodness, faithfulness, and deliverance.

In this passage, two phrases jump out. The first, "rest again," describes the response of those who know God and truly trust him for salvation. The second, "in the Lord's presence," describes the foundation for the first. As a person "walks" in God's presence, he or she can "rest" (relax) in his love and can live with confidence.

As you "live here on earth," know that you are living in the presence of your loving, holy, and almighty God. He is with you, guarding and guiding. You can relax in his love and live with peace.

He will shield you
with his wings
He will shelter you

HIS FAITHFUL

YOUR ARMOR AND

with his feathers

PROMISES ARE

PROTECTION

from PSALM 91:4

Give thanks to the LORD, for he is good!

His faithful love endures forever.

Give thanks to the God of gods.

His faithful love endures forever.

Give thanks to the Lord of lords.

His faithful love endures forever.

PSALM 136:1-3

41

- Do you remember young love? When it was over, you thought your heart would break.
- Do you remember being betrayed by one you thought was a friend? Angry and bitter, you wondered how to respond.
- Do you remember being the boss's favorite employee and then falling out of favor? Disillusioned, you seriously entertained thoughts of quitting.

GOD'S LOVE differs infinitely from human affection. His love lasts. Our God is not like other "gods" and "lords." He is *good,* perfectly good.

Twenty-six times in this psalm, the writer repeats the amazing truth, "His faithful love endures forever." Whether it was meant as a worship response or a poetic refrain, this phrase serves as a powerful reminder that should be repeated daily.

When grieving a loss, remember:
  God's faithful love endures forever.
When struggling for answers, remember:
  Your Lord's faithful love endures forever.
When feeling abandoned and alone, remember:
  The Father's faithful love endures forever.

I remember the days of old.

I ponder all your great works.

I think about what you have done.

I reach out for you.

I thirst for you as parched land thirsts for rain.

Come quickly, LORD, and answer me,

for my depression deepens.

Don't turn away from me, or I will die.

Let me hear of your unfailing love to me

in the morning, for I am trusting you.

Show me where to walk,

for I have come to you in prayer.

PSALM 143:5-8

42

THE PSALM WRITERS expressed themselves honestly to God—every feeling, from elation to despair. While fighting fear and depression, this writer turned to God in desperation. Remembering the Lord's mighty works of the past, he prayed for a miracle in the present.

Believers experience the whole range of emotions, the ups and the downs. The emotions are not wrong or sinful, they just are. But the response is critical. We can allow our emotions to pull us away from God or to push us toward him. In this case, the writer's depression moved him in God's direction. First he acknowledged his need and his total dependence on God; then he asked for God's guidance.

Don't allow fear and depression to drive you from the Lord. Instead, tell him how you feel and ask for his help.

The LORD is close

to all who call on him,

yes, to all who call on him sincerely.

He fulfills the desires of those who fear him;

he hears their cries for help

and rescues them.

PSALM 145:18-19

CALL ON

43

IN COMIC STRIPS and cartoons, masked superheroes answer calls for help from those in distress. They rush quickly to the rescue at the first sign of trouble. We know, of course, that such characters exist only in fiction and in our imaginations. But at times, we want the cartoons to be true, especially when facing complex issues, giant problems, and difficult conflicts. We want someone to hear our frantic cries and run to our side.

This passage in Psalms declares that, in fact, someone *is* listening. Not an imaginary hero with superhuman powers, but a real person with *all* power and authority (see Matthew 28:18) stands near, ready to save. And more than simply rescuing individuals from temporal plights, this person, the Lord almighty, saves for all eternity.

God knows your situation and your desires. He will fulfill your deepest needs.

"The Lord is near." He stands close and ready to help.

God listens for you. He hears your cries, and he will save you.

Two people can accomplish

more than twice as much as one;

they get a better return for their labor.

If one person falls, the other can reach out and help.

But people who are alone when they fall

are in real trouble. . . . A person standing alone

can be attacked and defeated,

but two can stand back-to-back and conquer.

Three are even better,

for a triple-braided cord is not easily broken.

ECCLESIASTES 4:9-10, 12

TWO ARE BETTER

44

I N THESE few short lines, Solomon highlights the value of friendships. Friends work together, help each other, defend one another, and encourage each other. In contrast, the person without any friends must face the world alone. We need friends to encourage and support us, to give feedback and hold us accountable, to console and counsel us, and to direct us to God.

At times, we may feel as though we would rather go it alone; after all, friendships require maintenance, and that means work. But God has created us as relational beings (Genesis 2:18), and he wants us to share his love with others, not to keep it to ourselves (1 Corinthians 13). And he promises to be our friend, one who "sticks closer than a brother" (Proverbs 18:24).

Friends are gifts from God. Receive his gifts with gratitude. And be a gift to someone who needs a friend.

Don't let the excitement of youth

cause you to forget your Creator.

Honor him in your youth

before you grow old

and no longer enjoy living.

ECCLESIASTES 12:1

REMEMBER

45

I T'S WONDERFUL to be young and filled with idealism and optimism, promise and potential. But young people have a limited perspective, and youthful excitement can deaden common sense and distort vision. Too often, while focusing on the *present* and on good *feelings,* they can forget God, the one who created them and loves them and the only one who can bring them safely to and through the future.

All too suddenly, the future is now, and individuals begin to struggle with the realities of aging. Then, those who have built on shaky foundations see and feel their lives crumble. The hard lesson, learned by each generation, is that a life begun without God often leads to a life lived without God, which leads to a life ending in pain and bitterness, without God.

In contrast, those who honor God while they are young focus their lives on doing his will—living the way he desires. Then, nearing the end, they look forward with hope to a glorious eternity with their Savior.

Clearly, this passage teaches that regardless of your standing—age, maturity, experience, expertise—God needs to be the organizing center of your life. Remember him and live.

Here is my final conclusion:

Fear God and obey his commands,

for this is the duty of every person.

God will judge us for everything we do,

including every secret thing,

whether good or bad.

ECCLESIASTES 12:13-14

THE ULTIMATE

46

"THE DUTY OF EVERY PERSON"—that's quite a statement. In this summary to his chronicle of his search for meaning and purpose in life, Solomon, the wisest man on earth, concluded that "the duty of every person" was to "fear God and obey his commands."

Solomon wrote this, under the inspiration of the Holy Spirit, looking at life from an eternal point of view. From a human perspective, people should seek pleasure, wealth, popularity, and power—success, according to the world. Solomon had achieved all of that and more; yet he summarized it all as meaningless, empty, vain. Solomon had learned that spending a lifetime pursuing those goals just leads to moral and spiritual bankruptcy. They don't satisfy, and they fade as quickly as the morning dew.

But looking at life from beyond finite human experience, Solomon could see that, in reality, only God matters. So he implores us to "fear God and obey his commands."

No matter how you rate on the world's scale, focus on God and his standard. He is all that really matters.

CONCLUSION

Learn to do good.

Seek justice.

Help the oppressed.

Defend the orphan.

Fight for the rights

of widows.

ISAIAH 1:17

GOD IS

47

THIS THEME runs through the entire Bible—God is concerned about justice in our world. It is also clear that he expects his people to encourage, defend, and plead for the needy in society. Thus, obvious personal applications flow from this verse as we consider the oppressed, fatherless, and widows with whom we come into contact. "What can we do to seek justice for them?" we should ask.

Beneath these words of admonition, however, lies another very personal truth, for this passage reveals a marvelous fact about God's nature. Because God wants justice, he will be on our side when *we* are oppressed and when *we* lose father, mother, or spouse. He will be fighting *for us* and will be *with us* through it all, encouraging us, defending us, and pleading our case.

So when you feel abused, abandoned, and alone, as though no one cares, remember that you worship a God of justice—supreme, almighty, the righteous judge—and he is on your side. And, oh yes, don't forget to encourage others with that truth as well.

It is God

who sits above the circle of the earth.

The people below must seem to him like

grasshoppers!

He is the one who spreads out the heavens

like a curtain and makes his tent from them.

He judges the great people of the world

and brings them all to nothing.

ISAIAH 40:22-23

OUR GOD

48

- A coup topples a government. The new dictator jails all who oppose his rule.
- A revered leader dies. A son succeeds and vows to rule the nation with an iron hand.
- A bloody civil war tears a country along ethnic lines, with leaders of both sides mourning their dead, claiming victory, and vowing revenge.
- An election sweeps a new party into power. The president-elect boasts of a mandate and promises broad reforms.

WITH EYES firmly fixed on this world, we can feel impotent in the face of military might, political power, and majority rule. Yet Isaiah reminds us that only God, the Creator and our Redeemer, truly reigns. His power knows no limit; he is sovereign and in control. Despite the rantings and ravings of the leaders of earthly nations, they have no true power and, ultimately, will be reduced to nothing.

Regardless of the political winds, keep your allegiance and attention on your sovereign Lord. He will bring you through.

Do not be afraid, for I have ransomed you.

I have called you by name; you are mine.

When you go through deep waters and great trouble,

I will be with you. When you go through

rivers of difficulty, you will not drown!

When you walk through the fire of oppression,

you will not be burned up;

the flames will not consume you.

For I am the LORD, your God,

the Holy One of Israel, your Savior.

ISAIAH 43:1-3

YOU HAVE BEEN

49

THROUGH the prophet Isaiah, God promised the people of Judah that he would be with them in every circumstance and through every trial. They were *his*. He had ransomed and called his people, and he would keep them safe and secure.

You, too, are God's child. Thus this promise belongs to you as well.

- What deep waters of tragedy and sorrow do you face? You are not alone—God is with you.
- What rivers of conflict and difficulty swirl around you, threatening to engulf you and carry you away? Don't fear—God will take you through.
- What fire licks at your heels? Keep walking—God will shield you from the flames.

Keep on, knowing that you belong to God, the *Holy One*, your *Savior*.

I—yes,

I alone—am the one

who blots out your sins

for my own sake

and will never

think of them again.

ISAIAH 43:25

WHEN GOD FORGIVES,

50

HUMAN FORGIVENESS often comes with hidden strings. We say we forgive, but later, at a crucial time, we yank the string and pull the offense back into view. Saying "I forgive you" comes easily, but truly forgiving and *forgetting* is much more difficult. Perhaps that's why we struggle with guilt, even after we have asked God to forgive. Knowing our tendency to store past offenses and hold grudges, we assume that God does the same.

But this passage proclaims that God will never think of our sins again. Does God take sin seriously? Definitely! Sin is so serious that it deserves the death penalty, eternal death (see Romans 6:23).

Does God *want* to forgive sinners? Certainly! God sent Jesus to take the punishment for sin, dying on the cross in our place. All who repent and trust in Christ can be forgiven (see John 3:17-18).

Can we trust God to forgive us? Of course! "Since God did not spare even his own Son but gave him up for us all, won't God, who gave us Christ, also give us everything else?" (Romans 8:32).

Release that load of guilt. Stand tall and breathe the sweet air of forgiveness.

When you will not be You Walk thro

burned up;
the flames
will not
consume you

FOR
I AM
THE LORD
YOUR GOD

the fire of
oppression

from ISAIAH 43:2-3

Sing for joy, O heavens!

Rejoice, O earth!

Burst into song, O mountains!

For the LORD has comforted his people

and will have compassion on them

in their sorrow.

ISAIAH 49:13

REJOICE AND

51

ISAIAH brought bad news and good news to God's people. The bad news was that they would be conquered, defeated, and taken captive by a foreign power. But the good news was that eventually the nation would be restored. The best news was that whether captive or free, God would be with them, giving them comfort and hope.

Do you feel hemmed in, trapped, a captive to your unrelenting schedule and assaulted by a host of enemies who threaten to steal your joy? Or do you feel desperate as you struggle with physical pain, financial demands, or interpersonal conflicts? Listen to God's Word. Isaiah tells us that the Lord comforts his people and "will have compassion on them in their sorrow." God hasn't forgotten you; in fact, he sees you right now and knows what you are going through.

Make your next move toward him, and then . . .

But he was wounded

and crushed for our sins.

He was beaten that we might have peace.

He was whipped, and we were healed!

All of us have strayed away like sheep.

We have left God's paths to follow our own.

Yet the LORD laid on him

the guilt and sins of us all.

ISAIAH 53:5-6

LOOK TO THE

52

HUNDREDS of years before Jesus' birth, Isaiah prophesied that our Lord would be wounded, crushed, beaten, and whipped. Looking back centuries later, we know that Jesus completely fulfilled all of these inspired predictions.

On the cross, Jesus took the punishment that should have been ours for our sins, bearing the scorn and pain and separation from his Father. Thus, now, because of what Christ did, we can be forgiven, know peace with God, and have eternal life.

When you feel weighed down by sin, stung by rebukes, burdened by cares, or torn by conflicts, remember Jesus and his sacrifice for you. He gave everything to bring you life. He loves you that much!

Is anyone thirsty?

Come and drink—even if you have no money!

Come, take your choice of wine or milk—

it's all free!

Why spend your money on food

that does not give you strength?

Why pay for food that does you no good?

Listen, and I will tell you where to get food

that is good for the soul!

ISAIAH 55:1-2

FULFILLING

53

IMAGINE a bright oasis with tall palms, clear springs, and abundant food and drink. Offering satisfaction and even *life,* this cherished spot in the sands would draw hungry and thirsty desert wanderers. Desperate and needy, they would expend every ounce of strength to get there.

Just as dry throats and parched lips yearn for drink and empty stomachs and starved bodies cry for food, spiritually starved and dry men and women strain toward sustenance. And like a glorious oasis, this passage gives hope. Here God offers satisfaction, renewal, real soul food—life. Other offers entice, but they prove to be mirages. This oasis is real.

Do you thirst? Drink God's Water of Life. Are you hungry? Pull up to his banquet table, and feast on his goodness.

AND FREE!

For my people

have done two evil things:

They have forsaken me—

the fountain of living water.

And they have dug for themselves

cracked cisterns

that can hold no water at all!

JEREMIAH 2:13

54

THROUGH the prophet Jeremiah, God strongly condemned his people for their actions. They had turned away from him, "the fountain of living water." "Living water" means a bubbling spring or a flowing river, pure, available, and life-giving.

People who live in the desert need water, and there's no better source than a spring or river. It would be strange indeed to ignore such an invaluable resource. Yet that is just what Israel did. Even worse, they had dug their own, leaky cisterns and were looking for water there instead. How foolish!

Note that God did not condemn their *thirst*—it is natural and even good that people need to be refreshed, cooled, and satisfied. The condemnation came for turning the wrong way to try to satisfy that thirst.

God's life-giving stream still flows nearby, available and free. Yet people still choose other ways to quench their spiritual thirst. Depending on their own ingenuity and work, they dig cisterns of materialism, relationships, popularity, power, religion, and so forth. But those cisterns leak, and their waters do not satisfy.

Are you thirsty for love? for significance? for purpose and meaning? for direction and guidance? for eternal life? Your thirst is good, but it needs to be quenched. Drink from God's stream!

*But blessed are those who trust in the L*ORD

and have made the LORD their hope and confidence.

They are like trees planted along a riverbank,

with roots that reach deep into the water.

Such trees are not bothered by the heat

or worried by long months of drought.

Their leaves stay green,

and they go right on producing delicious fruit.

JEREMIAH 17:7-8

55

*W*HERE do you place your trust? In family and friends? In money and possessions? In business? In government? Ultimately, even the dearest loved ones and strongest institutions will wilt and wither in the heat of this sinful world.

Not so with God.

A tree stands strong and green, bearing fruit year after year because a wise gardener planted it along a riverbank. Now its deep roots draw water from the life-giving stream that flows nearby.

In the same way, God knows what you need to nourish your soul—streams of living water—and he will plant you there if you let him.

Don't fear the heat or drought; trust in the Lord. You will be blessed. That's his promise!

Long ago the LORD said to Israel:

"I have loved you, my people,

with an everlasting love.

With unfailing love

I have drawn you to myself."

JEREMIAH 31:3

56

*A*S A CHILD, walking into your grandparents' home you were greeted with open arms and the familiar greeting, "Come and give Grandma a hug!" That's the picture here: God opening his arms and welcoming his children—drawing them to himself with kindness and love.

This statement of love and restoration comes after dark prophetic predictions of God punishing his people, allowing them to be conquered and captured. Certainly they deserved it; actually, they deserved even more. They had rejected God, worshiping idols instead, and had refused to listen to God's warnings through his prophet. No doubt they would be punished.

But God's punishment is always tempered with mercy because of his great love, described here as "everlasting."

The message is clear. No matter what you have done, God still loves you. As in the past, so in the present— he waits with open arms, drawing you with lovingkindness. Turn from your idols to the living God. Turn from your sin and indifference, and run to the Savior.

The young women will dance for joy,

and the men—old and young—

will join in the celebration.

I will turn their mourning into joy.

I will comfort them and

exchange their sorrow for rejoicing.

JEREMIAH 31:13

GET READY

57

HAVE YOU ever danced at a funeral? That would be unthinkable, absurd. Funerals are times of somber reflection, sorrow, mourning. We expect funerals to bring sadness and tears, not joy and celebration.

We mourn for many reasons, and each painful loss tears our emotions and causes us to regret past actions and missed opportunities and to wonder what might have been. Certainly nothing hurts more than the death of a loved one—we miss our fiancée or spouse or child or friend, and we long to hear that familiar voice and to feel the person's touch.

Through Jeremiah, however, we learn that God will turn "mourning into joy." That's God's plan. Because we know him, our ultimate destiny is heaven, and we have the solid assurance that one day all sickness, death, and sorrow will be banished—we will be perfect and complete. Actually, all of this earth, including our pain, is temporary, but our joy will last forever.

Whatever your sorrow, keep your eyes on Christ and gain God's eternal perspective. And then . . .

No, O people,

the LORD has already told you what is good,

and this is what he requires:

to do what is right,

to love mercy,

and to walk humbly with your God.

MICAH 6:8

JUST WHAT

58

*A*T TIMES, you may wonder what God expects. With the multitude of churches and wide variety of religious voices added to the messages from your personal study and your conscience, you may feel overwhelmed with duties and obligations. In this simple statement, however, the prophet Micah gives clear direction: (1) *do what is right,* (2) *love mercy,* (3) *walk humbly.*

Justice. Mercy. Humility. Consider the difference those qualities can make if actually applied. How would your life change? What would be the impact on your relationships? What would your community and nation be like if citizens lived according to this pattern? Most important, what would happen in your relationship with God?

In reality, the application of those changes in behavior occurs in the reverse order. First, we must humble ourselves before God, giving our total allegiance to him. Next, we must relate to others with mercy, loving and caring for our neighbors. Then, this genuine care will lead to standing for what is right in society and fighting against sin and injustice.

This summary by Micah also reveals much about God and how he deals with people. God hates sin, but he loves people, and he wants them to be saved (2 Peter 3:9). Rest in his love and follow his lead.

Where is another God like you,

who pardons the sins of the survivors

among his people?

You cannot stay angry

with your people forever,

because you delight in showing mercy.

MICAH 7:18

GOD LOVES

59

ONE IMAGE of God pictures him as judge and emphasizes his anger—as the righteous Sovereign, he judges sin and punishes sinners. Certainly this picture is true; God does reign supreme and just. And we should fear his wrath and obey his commands. This verse emphasizes, however, that although God lives forever, he does not stay angry that long. In fact, God *delights* in showing mercy.

In *this* image, God is like a loving father with a disobedient child. Knowing that he must punish, he would much rather have the child repent so that he can show mercy and forgive.

The phrase "the survivors among his people" refers to God's true children—people of faith (a small minority in the world). That's you, if you have trusted Christ as Savior.

So hear the lesson, child of God. Your Father loves you and stands ready to pardon your sin.

Don't be afraid. Don't run away in fear. Confess your sin and receive his mercy.

God blesses

those who mourn,

for they will be comforted.

YOU WILL BE

60

*W*HY? we silently shout to God as we stand by the grave of a loved one. Overwhelmed by grief, we question God's goodness and wonder how he could allow such suffering and pain. Death seems such a defeat. And that's not all: Each day brings a multitude of reasons for discouragement and despair—lost dreams, broken promises, hurt feelings, persecution, misunderstanding, disease, war, natural disaster. . . .

Yet Jesus could say that those who mourn will be blessed. And don't forget that Jesus would experience the death of a close friend, rejection by family and friends, physical and verbal abuse from religious leaders, disappointment with inconsistent disciples, betrayal by a close associate, and ultimately, an excruciating death on the cross.

Jesus knew that this life is not all there is and that those who trust in him will find deep comfort, profound peace, and unending joy in his presence.

Whatever the cause, let your mourning push you toward the Savior. You will be blessed.

The young women
AND THE MEN – OLD AND YOUNG
I will turn
INTO

will dance for joy

WILL JOIN IN THE CELEBRATION

their mourning

joy

from JEREMIAH 31:13

Look at the lilies and how they grow.

They don't work or make their clothing,

yet Solomon in all his glory was not dressed

as beautifully as they are.

And if God cares so wonderfully

for flowers that are here today and gone tomorrow,

won't he more surely care for you?

You have so little faith!

So don't worry about having enough

food or drink or clothing.

MATTHEW 6:28-31

61

OOD, drink, clothes—these comprise some of the basics of life. Why shouldn't we worry about them? No one wants to be hungry, thirsty, or unprotected.

The answer begins by understanding the difference between *concern* and *worry*. Concern means being aware of specific needs and then taking steps to meet those needs—concern leads to responsible action. It would be irresponsible and sinful, for example, for a father to be unconcerned about the basic needs of his family.

Worry, on the other hand, is extreme concern— concern gone to seed—an obsession with those needs. Filled with anxiety and fearing the worst, worriers nervously wonder about the future. They tend to spend more time filling their minds with ideas of the worst that could happen than working to make their dreams for the best that could happen come true.

The answer to the worry question is understanding that God is the ultimate source of everything good and that he loves us, knows our needs, and shares our concerns.

When tempted to worry about life's basic necessities, rely on this promise from Jesus: God will take care of you. As you live and work, trust him to meet your needs.

Not even a sparrow,

worth only half a penny,

can fall to the ground

without your Father knowing it.

And the very hairs on your head

are all numbered. So don't be afraid;

you are more valuable to him than

a whole flock of sparrows.

MATTHEW 10:29-31

YOU COUNT

62

ONE of the smallest birds is the sparrow—
and surely one of the most common and ordinary.
Sparrows come in many varieties and can be found all
over the world.

Jesus used this tiny and seemingly insignificant
creature to illustrate God's care for the earth and to
teach the value of God's most valued creation—human
beings.

How much are sparrows worth? In the world, not
very much. But God knows when each one falls. How
much are you worth . . .

according to the world?

according to God?

Whenever you feel hopeless, helpless, and worthless,
consider that you hold much more value than any
sparrow. God knows you, watches you, and cares for
you.

Mary responded, "Oh, how I praise the Lord.

How I rejoice in God my Savior!

For he took notice of his lowly servant girl,

and now generation after generation

will call me blessed.

For he, the Mighty One, is holy,

and he has done great things for me.

His mercy goes on from generation to generation,

to all who fear him."

LUKE 1:46-50

YOUR SAVIOR

63

THIS STATEMENT comes from Mary's inspired song of praise to God for being chosen as the one who would bear his Son. Although Mary didn't know all the details, she knew for certain that through her the entire world would be blessed as God fulfilled the covenant that he had made with Abraham centuries earlier (see Genesis 18:18).

Mary underscores three profound truths about God: He is "mighty"; he is "holy"; he extends "mercy."

Because of God's holiness, no sinful human being can stand in his presence; thus, all fall short of heaven (Romans 3:23) and are cut off from his love. Because of God's might, sinners (all people) stand condemned for their sin and face terrible punishment (Romans 6:23). But because of God's mercy, forgiveness, new life, and eternal life are available to all who believe (Romans 10:9-10)—through Jesus, God's only Son, born of Mary.

And God's mercy "goes on from generation to generation"—from Creation to now.

Hear this truth in Mary's song, and rejoice with her. God's mercy extends *to you*. Jesus came to earth, died, and rose again *for you*.

So he returned home to his father.

And while he was still a long distance away,

his father saw him coming.

Filled with love and compassion,

he ran to his son,

embraced him, and kissed him.

LUKE 15:20

64

IN THE HAPPY ENDING to Jesus' marvelous parable, the father runs to his prodigal son, welcoming him home. Note that the father sees the son "while he was still a long distance away." Thus, he must have been looking daily for his wayward boy. And when he catches a glimpse of the bedraggled and contrite young man in the distance, the father drops everything and runs to his beloved son. Nothing is more important than this homecoming, this joyous reunion.

The father represents God—loving, giving, and patiently waiting. And we, his wayward children, are represented by the son.

Where are you in the story? Perhaps you are ready to leave home—tired of the restrictions and rules, you want to go your own way. Maybe you are in the "distant land" (Luke 15:13), far from home and having a ball. Perhaps you are in the pigpen—broke, hungry, and painfully aware of what you left behind. Maybe you're headed back, rehearsing your speech of repentance. Or you may be in between those points in the story.

Wherever you are, your loving Father waits for your return. Standing at the edge of the yard, peering into the distance, he looks for that familiar form. "Filled with love and compassion," he is ready to run, to open his arms and welcome you back, to hug and kiss you, and to celebrate.

HOME

Jesus replied,

"People soon become thirsty again

after drinking this water.

But the water I give them

takes away thirst altogether.

It becomes a perpetual spring within them,

giving them eternal life."

JOHN 4:13-14

TAKE A

65

WHEN Jesus spoke with the Samaritan woman at the well, he offered her *eternal* life. Relating his offer to physical thirst, he described *his* "water" as a perpetual spring, quenching thirst forever. Jesus could make this promise because he was God in the flesh—the author of life and the giver of eternal life. And when Jesus makes a promise, we can be sure that he will fulfill it—all those who drink *will* live forever.

Are you frustrated with this world, its pain and struggles? Remember, this life is not all there is.

Are you thirsty for meaning, purpose, and significance? Remember, water from Jesus will quench your longings and deepest needs.

Have you visited numerous "wells" in your search? Remember, Jesus alone is the source of this eternal spring!

I am leaving you with a gift—

peace of mind and heart.

And the peace I give

isn't like the peace the world gives.

So don't be troubled or afraid.

JOHN 14:27

NEVER FEAR,

66

*F*EAR moistens our palms, buckles our knees, and chokes our breath. Debilitating fear makes cowards of even the strongest and most powerful warriors. Some try to fight their fears by ignoring them. Others mask their fears through anesthesia (alcohol and drugs) or false bravado (pretending that all is well). Some respond by rushing recklessly into danger. But the answer, the effective antidote to fear, comes from knowing the truth and knowing what lies ahead, down the path.

Jesus told his disciples that he was the Truth (John 14:6) and that heaven awaited all who trusted in him (John 14:1-4). Thus they need not fear, regardless of their circumstances, pressures, and troubles. Certainly these young men didn't know the future, but they knew the one who did—and he promised them peace.

What fears steal your hope and keep you awake at night? Trust the Savior, and sleep like a baby.

I no longer call you servants,

because a master doesn't confide

in his servants.

Now you are my friends,

since I have told you everything

the Father told me.

JOHN 15:15

WHAT A

67

IN THE MIDDLE of his last instructions to his disciples before he was betrayed, tried, and crucified, Jesus explained that they should see themselves as his friends, not as his servants. It was an important distinction. Good servants work hard for the master and are loyal and faithful. But they don't ask why. They aren't privileged to know the master's plans, reasons, and motives. They simply obey.

Friends, however, enjoy a close relationship. They share experiences and information. They know each other well, and they move together in the same direction.

Jesus had revealed to these men all that he had learned from his Father. They truly were his friends.

Twenty centuries later, we who name Christ as Savior also stand as his friends. He has given us the Bible, his written Word, to study and apply and the Holy Spirit to teach us (John 14:26). We can know the Master's business.

When you don't know which way to turn, ask God. He will answer because *Jesus is your friend.* When you feel all alone, turn your thoughts heavenward, remembering that *Jesus is your friend.* He's there when you need him.

But I will send you the Counselor—

the Spirit of truth.

He will come to you from the Father

and will tell you all about me.

JOHN 15:26

SENT FROM

68

JESUS is teaching the disciples about the Holy Spirit, the "Spirit of truth." Translated as "Counselor" or "Comforter," the Greek word literally means "one who comes alongside." So this title pictures one person coming close to another, alongside, to guide (as on a path in the woods), to advise (as a lawyer in a court of law), to counsel (as a psychiatrist or simply a trusted friend), to speak words of concern (as in a hospital room), or to comfort (as at a graveside).

Clearly, God sends his Spirit to help all believers. And he counsels and comforts by telling the truth about Jesus, assuring believers of Christ's true identity, forgiveness of sins, love, and salvation.

Do you feel lost, wondering which way to turn? You are not alone. The Holy Spirit stands beside you and will guide you God's way.

Do you feel accosted and accused? You're not alone. God's Spirit comes to your defense.

Do you feel confused, frustrated, anxious, or fearful? You're not alone. The Counselor is with you to give you hope and to tell you how to live.

Do you feel devastated by loss and overcome with grief? You're not alone. The Comforter is close, wrapping his arms around you and whispering words of love.

THE FATHER

It was not long after he said this

that he was taken up into the sky

while they were watching,

and he disappeared into a cloud.

As they were straining their eyes to see him,

two white-robed men

suddenly stood there among them.

They said, "Men of Galilee,

why are you standing here staring at the sky?"

ACTS 1:9-11

69

HY did the disciples stand and look intently into the sky? Maybe they were stunned and amazed at seeing Jesus ascend into the air through the clouds. They may have been saddened by his sudden disappearance and were looking anxiously for him to descend. Or perhaps they were confused and didn't know what else to do.

Whatever their thoughts or motives, however, two angels ("white-robed men") gave them the word. They could stop looking *up* and start looking *around* at the world and its needy people (John 4:35). They could stop waiting and start working to fulfill Christ's commission (Matthew 28:18-20). They could stop wondering and start living with the assurance that Jesus would come again, just as he had promised (John 14:3).

Although nearly two thousand years have passed since this dramatic event, the angels' message still stands—Jesus will surely return. That truth should continue to motivate believers. In fact, each day that passes provides another day to work for Christ and his kingdom.

Keep hoping, working, loving, sharing the Good News, and living for the Savior. He will come back.

Then Peter replied,

"I see very clearly that

God doesn't show partiality.

In every nation

he accepts those who fear him

and do what is right."

ACTS 10:34-35

FEAR GOD AND

70

*W*E'RE used to people playing favorites. Teachers have "pets," bosses have "fast-track employees," and just about everyone has a "best friend." And remember those days when kids would choose sides for playground games? The "good" players were chosen first, and no one wanted to be chosen last.

Considering our experience, we might assume that God acts the same way—that he favors certain people because of ability, personality, physical attributes, social standing, or another identifying characteristic. (Peter certainly felt that way—he was sure that Gentiles were unclean.) This assumption may lead us to wonder about God's feelings toward us and, perhaps, even to doubt our relationship with him.

But God revealed the truth to Peter: God doesn't act that way. That is, "God doesn't show partiality." Instead, he accepts people "in every nation." The only qualification for acceptance is that they honor and revere ("fear") him and obey him.

Are you feeling rejected, put down, or alone? Know that God accepts you, affirms you, and stands by you. And through his Son, Jesus, he gives you eternal life, regardless of your height, beauty, weight, strength, gender, talent, ability, or nationality. He has chosen *you*.

WE CAN

They help us

WHEN WE

and endurance develops

PROBLEMS

and

FOR

our confident

THEY

REJOICE

learn to endure

RUN INTO

strength of character in us

AND TRIALS

character strengthens

WE KNOW

expectation of salvation.

ARE GOOD FOR US

from ROMANS 5:3-4

Therefore, since we have been made right

in God's sight by faith, we have peace with God

because of what Jesus Christ our Lord

has done for us. . . .

We confidently and joyfully look forward

to sharing God's glory. We can rejoice, too,

when we run into problems and trials,

for we know that they are good for us—

they help us learn to endure.

And endurance develops strength of character in us,

and character strengthens our confident expectation

of salvation.

ROMANS 5:1-4

71

THIS profound passage teaches that those who know Christ have:

- justification—we are declared not guilty because of what Christ has done on the cross.
- peace—we are no longer at war with God.
- hope—we are assured of a glorious future.
- love—we are filled with God's presence.
- endurance—we can stand strong and persevere.
- character—we are honest, dependable, and filled with integrity.
- joy—we rejoice in God and his marvelous plan.

God sent these words, through Paul, to people familiar with struggles, hardships, and pain. And God knew that their suffering would increase tenfold. So he encouraged these beleaguered Roman Christians with these truths, to give them hope and joy.

- Are you lonely? God gives his love.
- Do you struggle with conflicts and worries? God gives his peace.
- Have you reached the end of your resources? God gives his hope.
- Are you suffering, in pain? God gives his Spirit, working in you to develop perseverance and character.

REJOICE!

For we are not our own masters

when we live or when we die.

While we live, we live to please the Lord.

And when we die, we go to be with the Lord.

So in life and in death, we belong to the Lord.

Christ died and rose again for this very purpose,

so that he might be Lord of those

who are alive and of those who have died.

ROMANS 14:7-9

YOU BELONG

72

ANTED: DEAD OR ALIVE! A poster with that inscription would usually refer to a notorious criminal. Yet this passage presents a curious twist of meaning for that phrase. Paul is stating that all believers are *wanted* by God (that is, they are desired and loved), dead or alive.

To be *unwanted* is to be rejected, left alone. Painful isolation brings silent tears and cries in the night. No hurt strikes deeper than that of abandonment. Solitary confinement is the ultimate prison punishment.

Thus, believer, you need to listen to God's truth shouted across the centuries—you are *not* alone. Whether living or dead, believers belong to the Lord. And to prove that assertion, Paul adds: "That's why Jesus died and rose from the dead!"

Think of it—God loved you so much that he sent Jesus to die on the cross for you. God loved you so much that he raised Jesus from the dead, and he now lives for you. You are not alone; you are loved.

As you live, he lives with you and in you. When you die, he takes you to live with him.

Now you have every spiritual gift

you need as you eagerly wait

for the return of our Lord Jesus Christ.

He will keep you strong right up to the end,

and he will keep you free from all blame

on the great day when

our Lord Jesus Christ returns.

God will surely do this for you.

1 CORINTHIANS 1:7-9

ENRICHED

73

THIS LETTER was difficult for Paul to write because the Corinthian church was struggling with conflict and division. Yet in the verses preceding these (1 Corinthians 1:4-6), Paul affirmed God's work for and in the believers there. They had been "enriched" in their "eloquence" and "knowledge," and they had every necessary "spiritual gift." In addition, Paul reminded them that God would keep them "strong right up to the end" and "free from all blame."

From this passage it becomes obvious that the Christian life depends totally on God. He calls, gives faith, saves by faith, confirms salvation, distributes spiritual gifts, strengthens, and keeps till the end.

God's favor is *undeserved*. No one can earn it—not in the first century and not today, neither the Corinthians nor you. That's grace. And God is *faithful*. No one holds on to God; he does the holding and keeping.

Regardless of your past sins or present condition, if you have trusted in Christ as Savior, God is working in you. His plan is to conform you to the image of Christ (see Romans 8:29), to present you "free from all blame on the great day when our Lord Jesus Christ returns." So stop struggling and start living for him.

BY GRACE

For Christ must reign until

he humbles all his enemies beneath his feet.

And the last enemy to be destroyed is death. . . .

When this happens—

when our perishable earthly bodies

have been transformed into heavenly bodies

that will never die—

then at last the Scriptures will come true:

"Death is swallowed up in victory.

O death, where is your victory?

O death, where is your sting?"

1 CORINTHIANS 15:25-26, 54-55

74

CHRIST, our risen Savior, reigns as the King of kings and Lord of lords. Against him no enemy can stand, not Satan or sin or even death.

It's natural to fear death. That insidious thief can appear without warning, at any time and in any place, robbing us of friendship, love, companionship, and joy. We fear for our own lives, but we also fear the death of those we love. Death looms as the certain but mysterious fate of every living creature. If only death were like a trip that one could experience and then live to tell others about. But no one returns from the dead.

But someone did. Jesus died and then conquered death, rising to life again. And he brings new life and hope and peace to all who trust in him.

In your sorrow, look to Jesus. He offers hope beyond the grave.

In your fear, turn to Jesus. He will quiet your storm and bring you safely to the shore.

In your pain, lean on Jesus. He defeated death and will take you through.

All praise to the God and Father

of our Lord Jesus Christ.

He is the source of every mercy

and the God who comforts us.

He comforts us in all our troubles

so that we can comfort others.

When others are troubled,

we will be able to give them the same comfort

God has given us.

2 CORINTHIANS 1:3-4

75

YEARS AGO, the chorus of a contemporary Christian song challenged Christians to "pass it on," to spread the message of God's profound love and incredible salvation to others.

In effect, that is what Paul is urging in this passage, explaining that one reason God comforts us is so we can comfort others.

So what comfort do we receive from God?

- When we feel lonely and isolated, God assures us of his presence.
- When we struggle against pressures and problems, God provides his power.
- When we despair of life on earth, God points to the hope of heaven.
- When we grieve over unbearable loss, God gives himself.

In the same way, we can comfort others—by being with them, helping, giving words of encouragement, telling of eternal life, pointing to the Savior.

Who needs *your* comfort? Think of how God has comforted you, and then . . .

IT ON!

In fact, we expected to die.

But as a result,

we learned not to rely on ourselves,

but on God who can raise the dead.

And he did deliver us from mortal danger.

And we are confident that

he will continue to deliver us.

2 CORINTHIANS 1:9-10

SET YOUR

76

OFTEN, on his missionary journeys, Paul would face desperate situations with no hope in sight. Reflecting back on one of those occasions, Paul could see that through the hardship God was teaching him and his traveling companions a valuable lesson: They were to rely on God and his power and not on themselves. Certainly, almighty God "who can raise the dead" could be counted upon to rescue them from any "mortal danger."

Whatever the situation, Paul could place his faith in God because he knew who God was and because he had seen God work before. Thus, he set his hope squarely on his awesome Lord and Savior.

What desperate circumstances confront you today? A doctor's negative report? Lack of resources? A broken relationship? Paul encourages you to learn what he had to learn the hard way—to rely on God.

Turn to him in your desperation. He "can raise the dead"; surely he can deliver you. Recall those special times when God rescued you in the past, and know that he will do it again. God "will continue to deliver" you.

You know how full of love and kindness

our Lord Jesus Christ was.

Though he was very rich,

yet for your sakes he became poor,

so that by his poverty

he could make you rich.

2 CORINTHIANS 8:9

YOU ARE

77

ESUS turns the values of the world upside down. He taught that those who lose their lives will find them (Matthew 10:39), the first will be last and the last, first (Matthew 20:16), and those who humble themselves will be exalted (Matthew 23:12). And this passage teaches that through Jesus' poverty, we can become rich.

In contrast, worldly values include winning, being first, and being exalted. In addition, the world's idea of being "rich" involves money, possessions, and power. No wonder the world finds it difficult to understand and accept Christ. To Jesus, true riches include forgiveness, peace, purpose, and eternal life.

The Lord Jesus Christ left "riches"—his power and the glory of heaven—to become "poor"—living as a human being, suffering scorn and abuse, and dying on the cross. Now, because of what Jesus has done, we can share in God's wealth.

Comparing yourself to the world's standard, you may not measure up, and you may feel insignificant, a failure. Yet, according to God's standard, you stand tall, a glorious success. Regardless of the size of your bank account, house, or pile of earthly goods, you are rich in God's grace. Stack God's riches next to the world's—the difference is infinite.

There is no longer Jew or Gentile,

slave or free, male or female.

For you are all Christians—

you are one in Christ Jesus.

And now that you belong to Christ,

you are the true children of Abraham.

You are his heirs,

and now all the promises God gave to him

belong to you.

GALATIANS 3:28-29

WHAT A FAMILY

78

IFFERENCES divide families, neighborhoods, communities, and nations. Differences in race, nationality, culture, social stratum, language, sex, and skin color push people from each other. The news media continually report stories of civil unrest, hate crimes, bigotry, terrorism, and "ethnic cleansing." The more we become a global village, the more, it seems, we splinter and divide.

This passage, however, describes a quite different situation. "In Christ Jesus" there is togetherness, oneness, unity. And instead of conflict, there is peace.

People of both sexes and all races, nations, and backgrounds are invited into God's blended family. Acceptance here is based only on Christ and what he has done. All who believe are welcome.

If you have ever felt the sting of prejudice and the loneliness of rejection, you know that this passage shouts good news. You are accepted and loved *now,* by God and your brothers and sisters, and you will live together in heaven *then.*

And because you Gentiles

have become his children,

God has sent the Spirit of his Son

into your hearts,

and now you can call God

your dear Father.

Now you are no longer a slave

but God's own child.

And since you are his child,

everything he has belongs to you.

GALATIANS 4:6-7

RUN TO

79

REMEMBER limping into the house after falling and scraping your knee? "Daddy, Daddy," you cried, hoping that somehow he would make everything right. Then Daddy would pick you up in his strong arms, wipe your tears, and hold you close. And it *did* feel better, and you felt secure, warm, and loved.

Many years have passed, but you still stumble and fall—in relationships, in business, in the home. And it still hurts terribly. At those times you long to have a loving parent hug you and kiss the pain away.

That's what it means to call God your "dear Father." When you put your faith in Christ, you became a child of God, born (1 Peter 1:23) and adopted (Romans 8:15) into his family. Now you have all the rights and privileges of a child of the King. You can approach God anytime with your needs, hurts, and concerns. Whatever your struggle, he will help. Whatever your question, he understands. Whatever your pain, he will comfort. He's your Father; he loves you.

Do you still act like a stranger or, worse yet, a slave, cringing before a tyrannical master? Know the truth— you can call God "Daddy"!

YOUR FATHER

How we praise God,

the Father of our Lord Jesus Christ,

who has blessed us with

every spiritual blessing in the heavenly realms

because we belong to Christ.

Long ago, even before he made the world,

God loved us and chose us in Christ

to be holy and without fault in his eyes.

EPHESIANS 1:3-4

80

THE WORD *chosen* connotes being specially selected. Choice foods are of highest quality; the top draft choice is seen as the best athlete.

Everyone wants to be chosen for the team or important position. Being someone's choice boosts one's self-esteem. Conversely, not being chosen can be interpreted as being ignored, passed over, or rejected outright.

So consider what it would mean to be *chosen* by God—selected, handpicked, pointed out—to be in his family, on his team.

That is precisely Paul's point in this passage. All those who follow Christ are God's *choice* people. In fact, they were chosen "even before he made the world." No wonder Paul says that we have been blessed "with every spiritual blessing in the heavenly realms."

When you feel neglected and rejected, when your self-esteem droops and you begin to feel unwanted and worthless, remember God's powerful statement through Paul—you are one of his *chosen* people. Praise God!

AND BLESSED

CHRIST

HAS MADE

BETWEEN US JEWS

BY

ONE

HE HAS BROKEN DOWN

THE WALL OF HOSTILITY

THAT USED TO SEPARATE US

himself

PEACE

AND YOU GENTILES

MAKING US ALL

PEOPLE

from EPHESIANS 2:14,17

For Christ himself has made peace

between us Jews and you Gentiles

by making us all one people.

He has broken down the wall of hostility

that used to separate us. . . .

He has brought this Good News of peace

to you Gentiles who were far away from him,

and to us Jews who were near.

Now all of us, both Jews and Gentiles,

may come to the Father.

EPHESIANS 2:14, 17-18

ENJOY

81

WHEN the Berlin Wall came down, the world celebrated. Tyranny had been defeated; a nation and families were reunited; peace had come!

Jesus is our "peace." He has removed the barrier separating us from God. We built that wall with our sin, our hostility toward God, and we lived in desperate darkness on the other side. But Jesus obliterated the terrible wall by paying the penalty for our sin on the cross. Before, we were at war with God; now we are at peace.

And this peace knows *no* barriers. Paul refers to "you Gentiles who were far away" and "us Jews who were near." *All* who trust in Christ "may come to the Father."

It is possible, of course, to live as though the wall still exists and thus miss the blessings of the Father. But how foolish. Now that the barrier is gone, don't let anything or anyone keep you from his love.

Stop fighting; the war is over.

THE PEACE

Because of Christ

and our faith in him,

we can now come fearlessly

into God's presence,

assured of his glad welcome.

EPHESIANS 3:12

WITH FREEDOM

82

CONSIDER how you would feel if you were summoned to the Oval Office to stand before the president of the United States. Certainly you would be apprehensive and shy, intimidated by the history of the room, the power of the office, and the presidential entourage. And certainly you would consider it to be a rare privilege to meet arguably the most powerful and influential person in the world.

With all that the office represents, however, the power and prestige of the president is nothing compared with almighty God, the creator and sustainer of the universe. Now consider how you would feel meeting *him* face-to-face.

But here's the incredible news: You can approach God at any time with freedom and confidence. Because of Christ's work on the cross and in your life, you can enter directly into God's presence through prayer. What an awesome privilege!

Freedom: You can talk with God about anything and everything. You can tell him about others, ask for help, and even admit your doubts and failures.

Confidence: You can talk to God boldly, without fear of condemnation for being honest and for being yourself. God wants to hear from *you.*

Whatever your need or situation, talk with God about it. He's approachable.

AND CONFIDENCE

Now glory be to God!

By his mighty power at work within us,

he is able to accomplish infinitely more than

we would ever dare to ask or hope.

May he be given glory in the church

and in Christ Jesus forever and ever

through endless ages. Amen.

EPHESIANS 3:20-21

INFINITELY

83

- Immeasurable
- Unimaginable
- Far beyond our thoughts
- Infinite

*W*E THINK we have it all figured out and believe that it is all under control. Confident of the possibilities, we predict what will happen in the days, months, and years ahead.

Then suddenly we are caught off guard as reality hits. Surprised by circumstances—diagnosed illness, natural disaster, broken relationship—we become painfully aware of our mortality and finite limitations. Then we realize that we actually have *no real control* and can only guess at what is to come.

But God knows. He knows the future and the past, and he knows us perfectly. He knows what we need and what will bring us joy. And that's good news! Think of it: We can't imagine the fantastic future that God has prepared for us. We can't even come close in our *asking.* His plans reach far beyond our wildest dreams.

When blindsided by life, look up and take hope. God's power works within you, and he is working for you, more than you can imagine.

MORE

Your attitude should be

the same that Christ Jesus had.

Though he was God,

he did not demand and cling to his rights as God.

He made himself nothing;

he took the humble position of a slave

and appeared in human form.

And in human form

he obediently humbled himself even further

by dying a criminal's death on a cross.

PHILIPPIANS 2:5-8

JESUS KNOWS

84

IT'S EASY to accuse God of not understanding our plight, especially when we hurt deeply and struggle for answers. God can seem so far away, so removed from the reality of our daily problems and questions. And during our pain we may question his love and justice; in desperation and anger we cry, "Why me?"
or "It's not fair!"

In this powerful passage, however, Paul reminds us that God is not aloof, above and beyond our struggles. In fact, two thousand years ago, Jesus, the fully divine Son, humbled himself and became a man—a living breathing baby, totally dependent upon his mother for food and shelter, vulnerable, small, and weak. Like other human children, the baby grew and matured to become a child and then a teenager and then an adult. Eventually, the Son's identification with us humans led to his suffering and death, for he was tormented, tortured, mocked, abandoned by his friends, and, finally, crucified. The least likely candidate, the innocent and pure Son of God, was executed like a notorious criminal.

Whatever your hurt, remember his. Not only does God understand and sympathize, he knows what you are going through—he lived it.

YOUR PAIN

And this same God

who takes care of me

will supply all your needs

from his glorious riches,

which have been given to us

in Christ Jesus.

PHILIPPIANS 4:19

85

God—holy, perfect, infinite, all-powerful,
      all-knowing, ever present, all-loving
will—in the future it will happen; it's a promise
supply—satisfy, fulfill, complete
all your needs—not your *wants,* but everything
      you truly *need*
from his glorious riches—unlimited power
      and resources
in Christ Jesus—the sinless Son sacrificed for you

THAT says it all. No matter how weak
and desperate you feel, hold on to this verse. God has
said it, and he will do it. Depend on him.

Work hard and cheerfully

at whatever you do,

as though you were working for the Lord

rather than for people.

Remember that the Lord will give you

an inheritance as your reward,

and the Master you are serving is Christ.

COLOSSIANS 3:23-24

EMPLOYMENT

86

*N*O ONE APPRECIATES ME!" Have you ever felt that way? Working hard behind the scenes, almost anonymously, you feel overlooked, neglected, taken for granted.

Employers make mistakes. Bosses become bossy. Supervisors reward incompetence. Teachers fail. Managers mismanage. That comes with living in a sinful world with fallible, sinful human beings.

Regardless of the job or work situation, however, God knows what's going on. (Note: Paul addressed this passage to slaves.) He perceives the attitude; he sees the work. He knows whether someone is giving the best effort or just getting by. Thus, God tells us through the apostle, we should work "for the Lord rather than for people." Certainly this would entail working hard, earning the wages, and being honest.

Understanding whom we serve can also free us from the trap of seeking earthly rewards and acclaim. No amount of money can match God's "inheritance," and no accolades can compare with God's "Well done!" That awaits all who trust Christ and serve him.

Regardless of the reactions of coworkers, classmates, and friends, focus on the Lord and work for him. His pay is worth living for.

OPPORTUNITY

Always be joyful.

Keep on praying.

No matter what happens,

always be thankful,

for this is God's will

for you who belong

to Christ Jesus.

1 THESSALONIANS 5:16-18

87

*T*HESE VERSES contain three commands that seem impossible to obey. The difficulty lies in the words *always* and *no matter what*. We wonder how we can possibly perpetually rejoice, pray, and be thankful, especially when encountering painful trials, inscrutable problems, and extreme conflicts. Yet this is what God wants us to do—it is his "will."

The last phrase of this verse—"belong to Christ Jesus"—holds the answer. When we consider Christ's work on the cross in the past, his intercession for us right now, and what he has promised to do for us in the future, we can be joyful and thankful, continually telling God our needs and seeking his direction.

Joy flows from knowing that God loves us. *Thanks* comes from knowing that God is working in our lives, in *each* and *every* circumstance. *Praying continually* is a natural response for those in close relationship with their Creator and Savior.

Note that God does not command us to be thankful *for* every circumstance. Instead, we are to praise him *in* each one. Regardless of what happens to us, God is with us working out his best for us (see Romans 8:28).

Focus on Christ, and live with joy.

And in his justice

he will punish those who persecute you.

And God will provide rest for you

who are being persecuted and also for us

when the Lord Jesus appears from heaven.

He will come with his mighty angels.

2 THESSALONIANS 1:6-7

RELIEF

88

THESE WORDS were written to first-century followers of Christ, who were living as a small minority in a culture violently opposed to their faith. Persecuted and harassed, many were rejected by family and friends and denied employment. Others suffered great physical harm. They looked for rescue. They yearned for justice.

And they heard the good news from Paul—*God is just*. Regardless of their present difficulties, eventually these believers would be rewarded for their faithfulness.

Pressed on every side, do you cry out for relief from trials and persecution and troubles? At times, a seemingly endless hoard of problems and pressures surround like a hostile army, threatening to attack and destroy. You can see no exit, no hope, only disaster and defeat. With thick clouds blocking the sun, you wonder if you'll ever see light again.

Now listen to this clear word from Paul—*God is just*. The all-powerful Creator loves. The all-knowing Sustainer understands. The supreme Ruler cares. And, one day, your Lord and Savior will return to take you home.

Eventually accounts will be settled, wrongs will be righted, and the righteous will be vindicated.

For at the right time

Christ will be revealed from heaven

by the blessed and only almighty God,

the King of kings and Lord of lords.

He alone can never die,

and he lives in light so brilliant

that no human can approach him.

No one has ever seen him, nor ever will.

To him be honor and power forever. Amen.

1 TIMOTHY 6:15-16

YOU WILL LIVE

89

THE ONE sure rule of life is that everything dies—grass, flowers, trees, insects, wild animals, pets, strangers, neighbors, and loved ones. No one escapes the death penalty. Accepting this chilling fact is difficult for some, especially the young, to whom a decade seems like forever. Eventually, however, each person must deal with his or her mortality. This unpleasant thought becomes a painful reality with the passing years. We long to live forever. But Paul reminds us that "[God] alone can never die."

But this statement provides hope. Satan will perish, as will all of God's enemies. At the end of the battle, only our Lord will stand. And because the King of kings and Lord of lords lives, he will do all that he has promised for those who trust in him.

Peace. Power. Purpose. Preservation. Eternal life.

While we cannot fully understand our God, we can trust him. And he has promised that although we will surely die, we will surely live again (John 11:25-26) in a place that he has prepared for us (John 14:1-2).

Whatever your struggle, take hope in this truth: God alone can never die, and he will take you home.

FOREVER

And that is why

I am suffering here in prison.

But I am not ashamed of it,

for I know the one in whom I trust,

and I am sure that he is able

to guard what I have entrusted to him

until the day of his return.

2 TIMOTHY 1:12

90

WRITING from prison, Paul declared his confidence in Christ. He was not ashamed of his situation or his Lord, and, despite his suffering, he continued to boldly proclaim his faith. Although Paul knew that he probably would be executed soon, he stood strong. Paul was convinced of the truth of the Gospel and of the strength and faithfulness of his Lord and Savior. He *knew* the one in whose hands he had placed his present and his future.

Living for Christ is not always smooth; in fact, the way can be rough. During those difficult times, doubts creep in. Fearing for our lives and considering our dire circumstances, we may lose sight of the Savior. But that's when we need him most.

Although not facing martyrdom in a Roman dungeon, you still may feel imprisoned and under assault, with no hope of rescue or release. That's when you need to refocus your attention on the Truth, remembering the one in whom you believed.

Christ will rule over all earthly powers. He will guard your faith and salvation. He loves you. He will bring you home.

JESUS
I S T H E

yesterday

Christ

S A M E

TODAY & forever

from HEBREWS 13:8

But then God our Savior

showed us his kindness and love.

He saved us,

not because of the good things we did,

but because of his mercy.

He washed away our sins and gave us a new life

through the Holy Spirit. . . .

He declared us not guilty

because of his great kindness.

And now we know that we will inherit eternal life.

TITUS 3:4-5, 7

91

ROTHER, have you ever been saved?" shouts the curbside preacher, and we cringe at his audacity and confrontational approach.

That is the important question, however, isn't it? Because if we *have been* "saved" (cleansed of all unrighteousness and forgiven of all our sin through the blood of Christ), then we *will be* saved (live eternally in heaven with our Lord).

The great miracle of this salvation is that we can do absolutely nothing to earn it. We gain forgiveness and eternal life through the generous kindness of God. His mercy and grace reach us wherever we are, whatever we have done.

Now justified, we stand clean in his presence.

When you ache . . . or stumble . . . or wonder . . . or cry out for justice, remember that you are . . .

SAVED!

Because God's children are human beings—

made of flesh and blood—

Jesus also became flesh and blood

by being born in human form.

For only as a human being could he die,

and only by dying

could he break the power of the Devil,

who had the power of death.

Only in this way could he deliver those

who have lived all their lives as slaves

to the fear of dying.

HEBREWS 2:14-15

92

EAR paralyzes, especially the fear of death.
Fearing for their safety, some people scarcely venture out into the world. They become imprisoned in their own homes. While most do not live at that extreme, nearly everyone, if honest, would admit to fearing death. It's always there, lurking beneath the surface. That's what motivates many to exercise endlessly and to consume large quantities of vitamins, trying, almost desperately, to postpone the inevitable.

The truth, however, is that each day, our mortal, flesh-and-blood humanity steals more of our youthful beauty and vigor and moves us toward the end. The reality of death is frustrating and frightening.

Those who follow Christ also die, but they don't die forever. They live again through the power of their risen and triumphant Lord. When Jesus died on the cross, he took the death penalty for all who trust in him. When Jesus rose from the grave, he conquered that fearful enemy. And his resurrection holds the promise that we also will rise.

Don't be enslaved to fear. Christ has set you free by destroying the power of death. Live with the joyful knowledge that you have eternal life.

Since he himself

has gone through suffering

and temptation,

he is able to help us

when we are being tempted.

HEBREWS 2:18

93

*W*HEN JESUS became a living, breathing human being, he became fully man with normal human needs and desires. Thus, as a baby, he had to be fed, dressed, held, and taught. Over the years, he grew and matured as a boy and a young man. As a normal Jewish male, Jesus experienced temptation. The Bible doesn't tell about his teenage years, but surely Jesus was tempted to disobey Mary and Joseph, to assert his independence, to lust, and to be filled with pride. Later, after his public baptism by John the Baptist, Jesus was led into the wilderness to be tempted severely, alone, face-to-face with Satan.

In all of these temptations, Jesus struggled, he suffered. Yet he resisted; he did not give in. He did not sin.

What temptations entice you?The first-century Jewish culture differed greatly from yours, but the basic temptations were the same: lying, stealing, hatred, pride, self-indulgence, worshiping other gods, materialism, and many more.

Picture Jesus in your shoes, in your situation—how would he respond when offered the chance to cheat, to stretch the truth, to check out the pornography and the other temptations?

Ask him to help you resist. Then make the decision that he would make.

HELP YOU

And let us not neglect

our meeting together,

as some people do,

but encourage and warn each other,

especially now that

the day of his coming back again

is drawing near.

HEBREWS 10:25

94

SOMETIMES people isolate themselves. When dealing with a difficult problem or struggling through a life-wrenching tragedy, they pull back from others and just stay away. It seems too painful to talk about, so they want to be left alone. Or perhaps they have sinned deeply and fear embarrassment or condemnation. Yet during those times of need and conflict they need others the most, especially friends who will listen, comfort, affirm, counsel, and point them to Christ.

That is exactly what the church should be—a place where believers encourage and strengthen each other, a place where people find acceptance and love and God's grace.

Evidently, according to this passage, some had gotten out of their churchgoing habit. They needed the body of Christ, however, considering the time in which they lived and their proximity to "the day of his coming back again"—Christ's return and the final judgment.

Today, we stand even closer to that day, and certainly we live in difficult times. More than ever we need others who know us and who know the Lord; we need to meet together regularly for worship, instruction, fellowship, challenge, and strengthening.

What keeps you from your Christian brothers and sisters? Don't stay away.

YOUR FAMILY

Jesus Christ

is the same yesterday,

today,

and forever.

HEBREWS 13:8

SECURE

95

CHANGE defines our world. Each day, a dazzling array of changes confronts us. Governments fall, children grow and mature, friends move away, storms uproot trees, new buildings replace old ones, colors fade, summer turns into fall, and technological advances render modern appliances obsolete. All these changes tend to undermine our feelings of security—we wonder what will last, what is solid, and who will be there. Our insecurity grows when once-close friends and associates renege on commitments and break promises, changing their minds and turning away from us. We wonder who we can trust.

Then we read this verse. Only nine words, yet it proclaims a marvelous truth: Jesus Christ, the divine Son of God who died on the cross to save us from our sins, then rose from the dead, and now lives, interceding with the Father on our behalf, *does not change.* In truth, he is the same as he has always been—loving, forgiving, merciful, and just. And, unlike the sources of many of our disappointments, Jesus is reliable—he keeps his promises. We can be sure that what he says, he will do. We can know that he will be *with* us and *for* us in the future, forever, in fact, just as he is today.

Feeling unsure or insecure as you face the continuous onslaught of change? Plant your feet and your faith on a solid foundation—your faithful Lord.

IN CHRIST

If you need wisdom—

if you want to know

what God wants you to do—ask him,

and he will gladly tell you.

He will not resent your asking.

But when you ask him,

be sure that you really expect him to answer,

for a doubtful mind is as unsettled

as a wave of the sea

that is driven and tossed by the wind.

JAMES 1:5-6

DOUBTS assail like gale-force winds, tossing us this way and that. We wonder what to do, which way to turn, what direction to take. We may even question our faith, doubting God's goodness or even that he is there. Like night storms, difficult circumstances terrify us, confuse us, and fill us with anxiety. But God's truth cuts through the darkness like the powerful beam from a lighthouse, providing warning, direction, security, and hope.

We aren't abandoned to our doubts and uncertainties; God says we can ask him, and he will answer . . . "gladly."

Do you want to know what to do? Do you desire to follow God's way? Do you need assurance of his presence and love?

Just ask in faith.

These trials are only to test your faith,

to show that it is strong and pure.

It is being tested as fire tests and purifies gold—

and your faith is far more precious to God

than mere gold.

So if your faith remains strong

after being tried by fiery trials,

it will bring you much praise and glory and honor

on the day when Jesus Christ is revealed

to the whole world.

1 PETER 1:7

97

CONTINUALLY persecuted for following the Lord, many of those to whom Peter wrote faced discrimination, verbal and physical abuse, and even torture and death. Peter's inspired message to these beleaguered believers reminded them that God was using their trials to refine their faith. Thus they should stand strong, keeping their eyes on Christ. In the end, all their suffering would prove worthwhile.

Modern persecution often comes in more subtle forms: social stigmatization, cynical sarcasm, interpersonal conflicts, and even legal restraints. Yet these also cause pain. And we can become weary of always defending ourselves and our Lord.

Who hassles you? What pressures and problems do you face? How are you suffering because you are a follower of Christ?

Whatever the persecution, know that God is using it to build your faith and to conform you to the image of his Son (see Romans 8:29). Let those around you know that your faith is genuine and "far more precious than mere gold." Take hope, knowing that all will be made right when your Savior is revealed.

STRONG!

The Lord isn't really being slow

about his promise to return,

as some people think.

No, he is being patient for your sake.

He does not want anyone to perish,

so he is giving more time

for everyone to repent.

2 PETER 3:9

GOD PATIENTLY

98

THE FIRST-CENTURY believers who read this letter were enduring terrible persecution. Often they must have wondered why God would allow them to suffer so much and why Jesus had not yet returned to rescue his own, to judge evil, to right wrongs, and to punish evildoers.

Today, we may have the same questions, especially when we see blatant disregard for and callous disobedience of God's laws . . . and when we suffer for our faith. This verse gives the answer—God's patience.

Jesus *will* return. God *will* punish those determined to live apart from him. Perfect justice *will* reign. But not yet because God is waiting, giving more and more people the opportunity to turn from their sins and to turn to him.

Whenever you wonder why God doesn't suddenly appear and eliminate all sin and suffering, think of his loving patience. And remember that he was patient with you, giving you time to hear the Gospel, to repent, and to trust in Christ as your Savior. Now, saved from perishing in your sins, you stand on the road to heaven . . . because of God's patience—his mercy and grace. What amazing love.

WAITS

But if we confess

our sins to him,

he is faithful and just

to forgive us

and to cleanse us

from every wrong.

1 JOHN 1:9

99

SIN becomes a terrible burden to bear, stooping the shoulders, bending the knees, breaking the heart. Yet men and women continue, day after day, trying to carry that soul-crushing load, desperately needing help . . . relief . . . forgiveness.

But why continue to struggle beneath the load of sin when the sin-bearer is near? Jesus, God's own Son, took our sins on himself as he hung on the Roman cross. He died so that we might live. He became sin so that we could be free from our own sin. All we must do is turn to him in faith, confessing our failures, disobediences, and shortcomings. With just a prayer, God lifts the load, forgives our sins, and makes us pure and free.

Feeling weighed down? Turn to Jesus.

AND FREE!

Look!

Here I stand at the door and knock.

If you hear me calling and open the door,

I will come in,

and we will share a meal as friends.

REVELATION 3:20

100

IN THIS powerful picture, Jesus stands at the door of the church and knocks. He wants to enter, to be welcomed in, to fellowship with the believers there. Note that although the Lord desires to enter, he allows individuals to open the door. Jesus doesn't force his will on them, pounding at the door, prying it open. Instead, he stands and knocks politely.

This church at Laodicea had become "lukewarm"; that is, they had allowed their passion for Christ to cool and had become enamored with themselves and their wealth instead. Eventually, Jesus was no longer with them. Thus, he stood on the outside, knocking, hoping to get their attention so that he might enter and change their lives.

Where is Jesus for you? Outside or inside? Is he a stranger, or do you "share meals" together? What concerns occupy your thoughts and desires? Relationships? Career? Possessions and power? Perhaps even survival? Do they threaten to push Jesus aside and move him to the fringe of your life?

Whatever your situation, know that the Lord is standing near. Through the din and demands, hear his gentle knock. Push through the clutter and open the door. Then welcome Christ and give him his rightful place at your table.

THE DOOR

SCRIPTURE INDEX